WHAT DOES IT ALL MEAN?

WHAT DOES IT ALL MEAN?

A GUIDE TO BEING MORE FAITHFUL, HOPEFUL, AND LOVING

RICHARD LEONARD, SJ

Paulist Press
New York / Mahwah, NJ

Dust jacket image by GD Arts / Bigstock.com
Dust jacket design by Dawn Massa, Lightly Salted Graphics
Book design by Lynn Else

Library of Congress Cataloging-in-Publication Data

Names: Leonard, Richard, 1963– author.
Title: What does it all mean? : a guide to being more faithful, hopeful, and loving / Richard Leonard, SJ.
Description: Mahwah, New Jersey : Paulist Press, 2017. | Includes bibliographical references and index.
Identifiers: LCCN 2016035147 (print) | LCCN 2016036922 (ebook) | ISBN 9780809106417 (hardcover : alk. paper) | ISBN 9781587686535 (ebook)
Subjects: LCSH: Christian life–Catholic authors. | Apologetics.
Classification: LCC BX2350.3 .L466 2017 (print) | LCC BX2350.3 (ebook) | DDC 239—dc23
LC record available at https://lccn.loc.gov/2016035147

ISBN 978-0-8091-0641-7 (hardcover)
ISBN 978-1-58768-653-5 (e-book)

Published by Paulist Press
997 Macarthur Boulevard
Mahwah, New Jersey 07430

www.paulistpress.com

Printed and bound in the
United States of America

Dedication

Gill & Robert, Christopher & Louise, Jane, Virginia & Andrew,
Jennifer, Simon, Helena & Jack, Diana & Bob, Poh Sim & Piers,
Louise, Eddie, Monique & Tony, Edith, Moira, Ed, Colleen &
Tim, Sarah & David, Diane & Sam, Gabby & Bastien, Theresa,
Bob, Lesley & John, Margaret & Neil, Bernadette & Patricia,
Paul & Danny, Peter & Anthony, Jim, Chris & Kevin,
Eileen & Frank, Virginia & John:
you have all helped me
clarify the questions and
strive for better
answers.

CONTENTS

CONTENTS

Contents

ACKNOWLEDGMENTS

Special thanks go to Mark-David Janus, CSP, Paul McMahon, and the team at Paulist Press for their continuing belief in me and my work, and for enabling me to talk to a very wide audience about faith and culture;

Brian McCoy, SJ, and the Australian Province of the Society of Jesus for the education and formation I have received and their ongoing support to do the "greatest good for the greatest number";

Rev. Dr. Stephen Hackett, MSC, and the Australian Catholic Bishops Conference, who understand that the ministry of communication involves various forms of the presentation of the word;

My Jesuit community at Lavender Bay, Sydney, for their forbearance and whose support and care, while I am either at home or away, provide a home base for a ministry often lived "with one foot in the air."

INTRODUCTION

Along with sales, feedback from readers is one of the rewards of the long hours involved in researching and writing books. Since *Where the Hell Is God?* was published in 2010, followed by *Why Bother Praying?* in 2013 and *What Are We Doing on Earth for Christ's Sake?* in 2015, I have been blessed to have enjoyed an extraordinary amount of correspondence and commentary.

The overwhelming response to these three books, almost all of which has been both positive and appropriately challenging, has been most moving. Since 2015, many readers have asked for a combined work with a good index so that they can easily access information on topics of interest to them. But this book is not simply a cut and paste of three works into one. As a writer, I did not plan to write the three books in the order they appeared—one flowed into the next. If I had planned the order, the last book would have been first, preparing the general ground for belief and unbelief, then confronting the biggest faith issue of all, holding on to a God of love in the face of suffering, and finally, exploring how we can pray with confidence to a loving God in the shadow of death and the valley of tears.

This volume, however, is not just a reordering of the text. It is much more than that because of the excellent questions, insightful challenges, and better insights my readers have offered me over the years. The content has been fully revised and augmented. However if some of the stories feel familiar, that's on purpose because, similar to the Lord, "without a story, I can tell you nothing."

WHAT DOES IT ALL MEAN?

As in the other books, I readily concede that some of the questions we will explore, especially those at the cutting edge of theology and the problem of evil, have been explored by other and better minds than mine and have come to very different conclusions. This is understandable since we are in the area of theological opinion and speculative theology. However, in the face of contemporary science, psychology, biblical studies, and personal experiences, traditional answers to complex questions of faith sometimes raise more questions than they solve. At very least, I hope to inspire in my readers a quest for answers that he or she may find more compelling and consoling so that together we become more faithful, hopeful, and loving.

PART I

THE CASE FOR
FAITH

1.

FROM THE AIR

Flying on a plane is both a joy and a risk for a priest. Depending on your point of view and experience, you might judge that I have been blessed or cursed to have to fly so much in my ministry as a Jesuit. Generally, I enjoy it, but I choose to fly under the radar—pardon the pun. I rarely wear clerical dress on a plane, mainly because Australian domestic and international flights are among some of the longest in the world and clerical collars are uncomfortable. Second, the sign of it repels as many people as it attracts; indeed, in secular Australia, it can attract unwarranted attention, wherein the attacker has no desire for a conversation, but simply seeks to spew bile on me.

Nonetheless, often when I am traveling in civilian dress, even before I can get my earphones firmly inserted, a fellow chatty traveler asks, "What do you do for a living?" Saint Ignatius was very keen on the art of the spiritual conversation, and so am I, but not in the sky. Ignatius knew nothing about twenty hours in economy class on planes! In my experience, once my inquirer finds out that I am a Catholic priest, and after accepting that I am who I say I am, the conversation goes in one of five directions.

The first category of responders is those who were educated by nuns, brothers, or priests, and unlike me, did not have a happy experience. This group is often made up of lapsed, collapsed, or ex-Catholics. For obvious reasons, if I cut across their tale of woe at this moment, I would only exacerbate the pain and prove their point about the uncaring religious officials they have known. My behavior would become part of their next story. It takes fifteen hours to fly from Sydney to Los Angeles, and four hours into the flight—somewhere over Fiji—I am regularly only up to the third grade with Sister Mary Agapanthus.

The second group comprises those who think I am deluded, that religion is nonsense, and that I believe in Santa Claus, the Easter Bunny, and fairies in the garden. (For the record, I don't believe in any of these three!) These travelers are as vehemently evangelical as any religious fanatic I have met. On one flight, one man, after giving me an earful about my psychological impairments, asked the attendant if he could be moved to another seat. Not only did I not get equal time to respond to my homegrown analyst, but he claimed that my religious belief was so clinicalized that he needed to move before I infected him with the bug! Mind you, when he got moved to a middle seat, I got two seats all to myself for twenty-four hours to London. God is good!

The third group is among my favorites. They are very conservative Catholics who, within three sentences of our conversation, know more about the state of my soul than me or my confessor. They have great gifts in regard to knowledge and prophecy, but few in regard to charity, which stems from the fact that I am not wearing a clerical collar. Therefore, they say things like, "Are you ashamed of your priesthood?" No. "Of your faith in our Lord and Savior?" No. "If you wore your clerical dress, you could provide a real witness for this plane, but you are one of those priests who want it all on your terms." Really? I point out that we are on a twenty-four hour flight to London, and I wonder if we would be having this discussion about my clothes if I were a judge, surgeon, soldier, policeman, or pilot. "A priest is a vocation, not simply a job," they reply. My fellow Catholic has not met the extremely dedicated surgeons and policewomen I have had the privilege of knowing. Then my interlocutor finds out that I am a Jesuit, and with a roll of the eyes, it is clear that my type of demon can only be cast out by prayer and fasting.

The fourth group is made up of my evangelical Christian brothers and sisters. Don't get me wrong, some of the finest Christians I know are evangelicals, but they can be a bit earnest, and their version of the eye of the needle is the only one through which all camels can pass. On finding out that I am a Catholic priest, they seriously ask me, "Have you given your life to Jesus Christ as your personal Lord and Savior?" "Well as a matter of fact I have," I reply. "Do you speak in tongues?" "I can, but I choose not to. I don't find it the most helpful form of communication." "Do you know the demands of living the life of the Lord?" Now somewhat exasperated, I say, "Listen mate, lifelong poverty, chastity, and obedience for Christ have to be a decent push in the right direction."

Actually, as I say this, I immediately think of the day I took my vows as a Jesuit in the chapel of St. Ignatius College, which overlooks Sydney Harbour. After taking my life vows of poverty, chastity, and obedience, my mother came and saw the magnificent sandstone buildings, the skyline of Sydney on the horizon, and the manicured lawns, which led down to the water on three sides of the property. My mother said, "If this is poverty, I want to see chastity. It is looking rather loose and fast to me." To which I replied, "We are very good on obedience." Actually, I hope we are good at all three!

The fifth group is the most serious: Catholics, Christians, other religionists, agnostics, atheists, humanists, and everything in between who are as scandalized as I am by the clergy sexual abuse crisis and its cover-up by Church officials. Some of these conversations have been worth having, although, as the only priest some of these people have met recently, you could be forgiven for thinking that I had personally committed these crimes and covered all of them up myself. Pent-up rage is often indiscriminate, for we never know when we are going to get another opportunity as good as this one to vent our spleen. We will return later to the sexual abuse crisis.

A few years ago, the experience of these conversations was so mixed that, when I received my doctorate in cinema studies, I changed my frequent flyer profile from "Father" to "Doctor." On my next long-haul flight from Los Angeles to Sydney, the customer service manager came down to me at row 57. After welcoming me as "one of our platinum frequent flyers," she said, "If there is anything that we can do to make your flight more enjoyable, don't hesitate to ask." So I did. "An upgrade would be nice," I said. She laughed, and walked back to the front of the plane. Her definition of "anything" did not extend that far.

On my next flight to London, down came the customer service manager again, to greet me at row 41 and to make a request. "Dr. Leonard," he said, "there is a lady in first class who may need your attention." I explained that, if she was having trouble selecting between the first release or premium movies, then I was her man. In fact, I thought I should get on the PA system and guide everyone through the entertainment offerings. However, if she was sick, I said, I would certainly not be helpful. As he walked away in search of a more immediately useful doctor, I had to stop myself from calling out, "However, if she goes to God, come back, because I know the prayers for the dead by heart." I restrained myself.

Of all the conversations I have had on planes, however, one of the most memorable led to this book. In 2013, I was flying from New York City to Los Angeles. As I settled into row 44, next to me was a very friendly young man, Thomas, who asked me what I did. I told him. He had been Catholic. I noted his emphasis was on the past tense, but said nothing. He wasn't sure about anything to do with faith and spirituality. I told him I was a Jesuit, which led him to tell me that he had been an undergraduate at Georgetown University and that he stayed in touch with one of the Jesuits who had lectured him. This priest had given Tom two books by another Jesuit priest. He couldn't remember the author's name but only the titles. I explained there were eighteen thousand Jesuits in the world and we write a few books, but try me: *Where the Hell Is God?* and *Why Bother Praying?* "Do you know them?" he asked. I looked around for the candid camera. "Yes, I know them very well; I wrote them." He would not believe me until I showed him my business card. This scene was unbelievable.

Thomas and I had a long and engaging conversation about the issues my two books had raised for him, and for me. Although we were as discreet as we could be, some of our fellow passengers must have wanted an emergency landing because of the advanced theology seminar happening at the back of the plane. Tom, who was thirty, was a highly educated person—an Ivy League graduate. He was also a serious humanitarian, working in Third World countries for Habitat for Humanity during several summer holidays. His wrestling with belief, theology, prayer, and the problem of evil came out of personal experiences. He told me that as much as he liked my earlier books and found them accessible and helpful, they did not address a fundamental issue for him and most of his friends: the why of belief. "We just get worn down by the growing chorus of people who say 'religion is all nuts and you can be a good person and make a difference in the world and not believe anything more than that.' And to say that the Catholic Church has made it very easy to leave in recent years is an understatement." However, Tom wanted more than that. "I can't simply believe that my life and, even more, the people whom I have seen in action with the poorest of the poor amount to nothing more than the here and now. There must be more purpose to life than that, or at least I hope so." The clincher for me was when he said, "I like reading the Gospels and what Jesus had to say on many things. I also think that Paul and others in the New Testament offer great lessons for life, but I guess what I am struggling with is what are we actually doing on earth, for Christ's sake?"

As soon as Tom said "for Christ's sake," he apologized, fearing he had offended me by swearing. Not at all! Everything that every baptized person does is meant to be "for Christ's sake." The fact that it has become a throwaway cuss line does not rob the phrase of its original meaning for me. "Why should the devil get the best tunes?" said William Booth, or depending on who you talk to, Charles Wesley, his brother John, or George Whitfield.

Maybe it was providence that I was slow on the uptake with my earphones and met doubting Thomas. As with all sincere searchers, Tom's questions were very good, and like another revelatory event that was shrouded by the clouds, "it was very good to be there."

Little did we know where the journey would lead us. Tom and I stayed in contact after that eventful tour through the clouds, meeting again in Sydney and New York City, this time with his girlfriend, Sophie. She was from a Catholic background, and as intelligent and humane as he was. By the end of that year, they announced their engagement. I received a phone call. "Father, when are you next going to be in New York? We would like you to be the celebrant of our wedding. We have decided to have a Nuptial Mass." Tom had come a long way in nine months, and this was one of only two weddings in my ministry where the date was arranged around my availability. It was one of the most joyful

Nuptial Masses I have ever done and was, possibly, only eclipsed by presiding at the baptism of Thomas Patrick IV earlier this year.

So these pages are for all the doubters and searchers I know; those who—like me—ask hard questions of Christianity and are often impatient for answers. We are fellow travelers on the adventurous journey of faith.

2.

THE COMMON GROUND

With the exception of Alain de Botton, my experience of listening to lectures by the new aggressive atheists like Sam Harris, Richard Dawkins, Daniel Dennett, and the late Christopher Hitchens leaves me with no hope, even while agreeing with some of their criticisms. Their take-no-prisoners approach is so regularly built on cynicism, raw anger, and trading in stereotypes, that I have come to conclude that they can be as fundamentalist and seemingly infallible as the religious edifices they build up to knock down. At gatherings of atheists, religion is not the only tyranny in the room.

It is a pity that the poster boys for aggressive atheism are so unlikeable. In passing, I note that there are presently next to no women leaders emerging out of this movement. Unrelenting negativity is a trial for everyone, and when applied to people who attack religion, it leaves me asking, I know what you are against, but what are you for? If all religion died, then what will take its place? Many aggressive atheists would say "being rational," which supposes that every position, other than their own, is irrational, but more on this later.

Whether some people like it or not, religious belief plays a very important role in nearly every society on earth. It needs to be said at the outset, however, that you do not have to be religious to be a moral person. Some of the finest-living people I know are atheists or agnostics or secular humanists. Clearly, religion does not have the morality market cornered. The clergy sexual abuse crisis proves that once and for all. There is enough hypocrisy to go around for everyone. While it was once understood that living the moral life was primarily promoted in terms of earning heaven and avoiding hell, much more nuanced developments in moral theology over the last fifty years or more have moved away from the reward/punishment paradigm to Christians living out what we believe as a response to Christ's invitation to have life and live it to the full.

Like all humanity, we often sin and fail, but we try to be moral because we are drawn by love, not driven by fear. However, it is striking how most aggressive atheists prefer to keep referencing the reward/punishment paradigm as the only dominant one in Christianity today. Along with many fellow Christians, I have long left behind the punishing policeman-God, with the long white beard in heaven, the "sky Daddy," ever ready to catch me out and send me to the fires of hell. Theology has positively developed, but that does not fit our opponent's preferred narrative and agenda.

Sometimes, I believe that some aggressive atheists are railing against their Sunday school teachers from the 1950s. They are entitled to do so, but most Christian theology has matured in the light of contemporary biblical studies, psychology, social sciences, and even in the shameful face of the criminal behavior of the worst of our members. From my experience, aggressive atheists resent it when people state, "Well, we certainly used to preach the position you have just outlined, but we don't anymore." Furthermore, in outlining a more recent or nuanced theological position than the one just presented, it is dismissed as "how very convenient," or "that's just your opinion," or "well, you held the old belief for a very long time." Apparently, for some of our detractors, no matter what new insights now inform our faith and its articulation, we are not allowed to move from the position that they seek to attack.

Some atheists argue as though all religions are monolithic in their condemnation of the modern world, their oppression of human rights, and their negativity to all social developments. This stereotype might once have been more true of mainstream Christianity, but it is far from true now.

Believers and atheists can find common ground in regard to the love of others and the love of self. Most people want many of the same things for the world: kindness, truthfulness, care for the earth, justice, peace, and love, just to name a few. We are sometimes divided over how we can best realize these things, and are always divided over whether our moral choices and ethical behavior have an impact beyond the here and now. Nevertheless, the fastest growing group in Western society is that which holds no religion at all. Within this group, the rise of those who are antireligion, secular humanists, or aggressive atheists is changing the discussion about what we believe, how we live out that belief, and the context within which we share values.

DIALOGUE WITH ATHEISTS

We need to take our atheist friends very seriously. Believers ignore, resent, or dismiss them at their peril. Again, we are in good company. On October 1, 2013, *La Repubblica*'s founder, Eugenio Scalfari, a public atheist, interviewed Pope Francis:

> "Some of my colleagues who know you told me that you will try to convert me." [Francis] smiles again and replies: "Proselytism is solemn nonsense, it makes no sense. We need to get to know each other, listen to each other and improve our knowledge of the world around us. Sometimes after a meeting I want to arrange another one because new ideas are born and I discover new needs. This is important: to get to know people, listen, expand the circle of ideas. The world is crisscrossed by roads that come closer together and move apart, but the important thing is that they lead towards the Good.... Each of us has a vision of good and of evil. We have to encourage people to move towards what they think is Good."[1]

Apart from those who call us insane, poisonous, and dangerous, not all of our detractors wish us ill. They just cannot or will not accept that any claim to religious belief fulfills their definition of rationality. Some atheists do not reject the notion of God outright, but they find the ideas about a God—any God—proposed so far in the human community totally unsatisfactory, both intellectually and personally. In fact, I readily concede that, in regard to every God outside of the Abrahamic tradition, I am a respectful atheist myself.

Against what most Christians would think of atheists, I argue that some of their challenges to religious bodies are very good indeed: demanding greater clarity in our thinking; demanding a case for the rationality in religious belief; questioning the right of religious groups seeking the case to have influence over laws, behavior, and ethics beyond their own faith community; and placing the spotlight on whether we practice what we preach.

No one likes scrutiny. "If you, O LORD, should mark iniquities, Lord, who could stand?" (Ps 130:3). Although the account of ourselves is sometimes demanded in the most provocative and accusatory of ways—and may indeed come from those who mean us harm—it does not take away from the fact that being asked to account for ourselves is fit and right. Jesus himself believed in such transparency: "For nothing is covered up that will not be uncovered, and nothing secret that will not become known. What I say to you in the dark, tell in the light; and what you hear whispered, proclaim from the housetops" (Matt 10:26–27). Furthermore, Jesus was the model of openness: "I have spoken openly to the world; I have always taught in synagogues and in the temple, where all the Jews come together. I have said nothing in secret" (John 18:20).

We recall that Jesus' first disciples were sent out to a hostile world and had to pay a price—sometimes the ultimate price—to witness to Christian faith, hope, and love. For some of us, who have become so used to Christianity being afforded respect, it can be disconcerting and dispiriting to encounter people hostile to the way, truth, and life that brings us meaning and hope. We might need to toughen up in dealing with the world, because Jesus never told us to sit at home and wait for the world to come to us on our terms, or to go out to it when it is ready to receive us with open arms. Jesus sent his earliest disciples out to a world that martyred them; he sends the majority of us out to an increasingly tough environment for religious faith, where we have to stand up for our words and ideas, our values and ethics.

While as Christians we should not seek an easy ride in accounting for our belief, one thing that is admirable about most atheists is the sheer confidence with which they support their judgments that there cannot be, and is not, a higher power—anything bigger, greater, or more intelligent in the universe—that many people call God. The same seemingly unshakeable self-confidence can also be on our side of the belief/unbelief divide too: God exists! We know it. End of story. Some believers go further and state that, at best, doubters are mistaken and that they will be damned for all eternity. Even in classical theology this position is wrong. While we are called to make right judgments in the light of faith in regard to thoughts and behavior, God alone is responsible for salvation and knows the reasons for someone's unbelief.

Personally, I find the apparent infallibility of both positions confronting, even unsettling. I have a deep and searching faith in and about God. I do not have a deep and searching certainty. Furthermore, I remain open to my faith in God developing, growing, and deepening as I reflect on the mysteries before me, both human and divine. In good company with St. Anselm, I have a faith that seeks to understand.

ST. THOMAS MORE (1478–1535)

Because how we live will always be more eloquent than what we say, let's consider the patron saint of respectful conscientious dialogue: Thomas More.

Hilary Mantel won many awards for her novel, *Wolf Hall*, about the fortunes of the Seymour family in England from 1500 to 1535. It is beautifully written and wonderfully researched, but Thomas More should sue for defamation. At Mantel's hands, More is not *A Man for All Seasons*, the title used by Robert Bolt for his play and later the film. The phrase was coined by More's contemporary Robert Whittington in 1522: "More is a man of an angel's wit and singular learning…a man of marvellous mirth and pastimes, and sometime of as sad gravity. A man for all seasons. " In Mantel's hands, More is only a man of deepest winter, a religious zealot responsible for many more deaths in God's name than his own. Luckily for Thomas's memory, Mantel's account of him owes more to the portrait of a contemporary religious suicide bomber than to a complex Renaissance man. His own son-in-law, William Roper, wrote the first laudatory biography about him, and this was done in honor of the man who left the family broke, disgraced, and in personal danger! I know whose judgment, I think, is closer to the actual subject.

Thomas More was indeed a complex man. He was twice married, first to Jane Colt in 1505. They had four children. When Jane died in 1511, he remarried, this time to a widow named Alice Middleton, who had a daughter from her first marriage. Thomas and Alice never had any children of their own. Sadly and revealingly, it is rare enough for a married man to be canonized a Catholic saint, but to be seemingly happily married twice, and after everything you put them through, to have the lifelong devotion of your children and even your in-laws is in itself a miracle.

More's story is familiar. King Henry VIII of England wanted to divorce his wife, the devoutly Catholic Catherine of Aragon. The pope would not dissolve the bond, so Henry worked to end the pope's authority over the church in England, which eventually became the Church of England. To do this, Henry needed the approval of the Peers and the Parliament. The king regarded his chancellor, Sir Thomas More, as a loyal friend. But by 1530, Henry required the English clergy to take oaths of allegiance to him as "Supreme Head of the Church in England." Not long after, Thomas More resigned his post. When Henry insisted that all Peers sign the Act of Succession—recognizing his powers over church and state, as well as his new marriage—More refused. In 1535, he was tried, found guilty of treason, and beheaded.

Although Bolt deserved all the awards he won for his play and film *A Man for All Seasons*, the last third of this work was not primarily written by him. It is a masterful editing of the actual transcripts of the trial of Thomas More, who by today's terms was England's prime minister. The trial lasted one day within Westminster Hall, July 1, 1535. The outcome of the jury's fifteen minute deliberations was never in doubt. To have found More not guilty would have incurred Henry's wrath, so it was a show trial in every sense.

The Duke of Norfolk then offered More a final chance to escape with his life: "You see now how grievously you have offended his Majesty; yet he is so very merciful that if you will lay aside your obstinacy, and change your opinion, we hope you may obtain pardon and favor in his sight." More replied—"stoutly," according to reports, that he appreciated the offer, "but I beseech Almighty God that I may continue in the mind I am in, through his grace, unto death."

More said in his defense that when the king asked him for his opinion about the divorce, he said that the state had no authority to dissolve the marriage. Stating the truth of the law, he contended, can hardly be treasonous. The Duke of Norfolk said, "Thomas, look at these names! Why can't you do as I did and come with us, for fellowship!" "And when we die," More replied, "and you are sent to heaven for doing your conscience, and I am sent to hell for not doing mine, will you come with me, for fellowship?"

Thomas More was found guilty and sentenced to be "drawn on a hurdle through the City of London to Tyburn, there to be hanged till he should be half dead; then he should be cut down alive, his privy parts cut off, his belly ripped, his bowels burnt, his four quarters sit up over four gates of the City and his head upon London Bridge." Henry VIII had this commuted to a simple beheading.

Of the many modern lessons from St. Thomas More's witness to belief, three stand out: the importance of silence, being prepared to die rather than wanting to be killed, and giving the best possible interpretation to your opponent's conscientious convictions, while demanding the same for your own.

More ended his life with a simple eloquence: "I am commanded by the king to be brief, and since I am the king's obedient subject, brief I will be. I die His Majesty's good servant, but God's first." The more we disagree, the more we should find ways to have respectful disagreements. There is a huge difference between free speech and hate speech.

3.

FREEDOM TO BELIEVE
AND NOT BELIEVE

We have moved on since the sixteenth century, and religious freedom is one of the great victories attained. In our contemporary pluralistic democracies, Christians always need to defend religious freedom, including the right not to believe. Atheists and agnostics have a right to disagree with everything we hold to be true, and all conversations should be marked by dignity and respect on both sides of the debate about belief and unbelief. The same applies to the way some Catholics and Christians talk to each other, especially in the blogosphere, where some so-called defenders of orthodoxy know everything about theology except that charity is the mother of all virtues!

Certainly, some nonbelievers could not care less about theology. Affording us the same rights, they are happy for us to believe whatever we want, even though they argue that we are irrational and deluded in what we hold to be true.

Their objections are more about the often privileged status religions can have in society in regard to a few legislative exemptions and taxation. While those days are in the past for most societies, it is unfortunate that some of our detractors ignore the contribution religious groups make to cost-effective, not-for-profit, accessible education, healthcare, and welfare. Every day, we work with the sick and dying, the poor, refugees, migrants, asylum seekers, the disabled, those with HIV/AIDS, convicted criminals, and many others who live on the fringes of society. Some of our detractors would soon notice these good contributions if we began not to do them.

They object also to the way religion, especially Christianity, is enshrined in our Western culture and laws. We cannot rewrite history, and while this influence is changing in the Western world, it remains true that in a democracy, the majority's worldview should be reflected in its laws and customs. Interestingly, many Christians would prefer to see more Christian ethics enshrined in recent legislative movements. It seems that none of us are content!

In order to have an informed discussion or dialogue between atheists and Christians, a few important ground rules need to be established.

NOT ALL CHRISTIANS ARE THE SAME

While Christians all believe in Christ as the Way, the Truth, and the Life, they have very different theologies and ideas regarding that belief. Many atheists criticize Christians for taking the Bible literally. I do not believe the Bible is the literal word of God and, since the Second Vatican Council, nor does the Catholic Church. Our Sacred Scriptures are not a book of scientific facts; they reveal religious truth, and they cannot err in what we need for our salvation.

Genesis, for example, does not tell us anything about science. It tells us about theology—that God is the ultimate author of creation. Therefore, Catholics, the largest group of Christians in the world—1.2 billion of us—do not, officially, believe the world was created in seven days six thousand years ago. As Pope Benedict taught, "On the one hand, there are so many scientific proofs in favour of evolution which appears to be a reality we can see and which enriches our knowledge of life and being as such. But on the other, the doctrine of evolution does not answer every query."[2]

Our atheists and agnostic friends may like to think that all Christians take the Bible literally, but Catholics don't; nor do many of the other, older mainstream Christian denominations.

17

SCIENCE AND RELIGION

Some aggressive atheists claim that believers cannot have faith in both God and science—that we have to choose. However, no matter what they say, we do not have to choose between science and faith. Science asks how we came to be here. Faith asks why we are here in the first place. Science questions the mechanics. Faith addresses the meaning. They are very different questions. While respectful of those who do not need to address issues of meaning outside their own existence within the natural order, I am certainly joined by many who are not one of them.

First, while it is true that there may be a majority of contemporary scientists who have no faith in God, it is not true to say that science and Christian faith always cancel each other out. Copernicus, Napier, Francis Bacon, Galileo, Descartes, Pascal, Leibniz, Newton, Sedgwick, Main, Mendel, Pasteur, Stokes, Marconi, J. J. Thomson, Bragg, Heisenberg, Mott, Eccles, Barton, and Robert Boyd are just a few Christians who are among the most famous scientists whom the world has known, even though some of them were criminally persecuted for their science by religious groups, including the Catholic Church, in particular. It is also inaccurate simply to say that in their day atheism was not a viable option. That may be arguable of the medieval and Renaissance scientists, but Halley and Maupertuis were well known for their arguments against any deity in the seventeenth century, and from the Enlightenment onward, atheism among scientists gained wide currency. Therefore, most of the men mentioned above had choices in regard to religious belief.

Furthermore, there are also world-famous contemporary scientists who have religious faith. Just to name a few: Nobel Prize physicist Antony Hewish; Sir John Polkinghorne, a professor of mathematical physics at Cambridge and also a priest of the Church of England; Francis Collins, a physical chemist, a medical geneticist, and the former head of the Human Genome Project; Templeton Prize winner, biochemist, and Church of England priest, Arthur Peacocke; and Nobel Laureate in medicine and physiology, Sir Ernst Chain.[3]

Many of these and other Christian scientists hold that there is such balance in creation leading to the evolution of human life and self-consciousness that there must be an intricate intelligence presiding over its order and development, which we call God. Some scientists go further and argue that the cause of the world is, by definition, scientifically supernatural—that it came out of nothing. That is what the Big Bang theory is about—it just happened. Theists hold that the Big Bang did not come out of nothing but from the primary cause—God. Atheists usually retort that if God is the cause of the causation, which produced the origin of the universe, then who created God? We hold that if one is going to be the Creator, God, then by definition that Creator cannot be created. God is. A growing number of atheists argue against the Big Bang theory by claiming that there are probably many other universes besides ours. However, at this stage, that is an unproved theory.

Other scientists argue for God on the basis of the extraordinary amount of biological information encoded into every organism on the earth, and not just in its detail and complexity, but in that so many elements had to combine in synchronicity for the created order that we now know to emerge. The scientific evidence would establish that every living thing has an internal cause and/or an external effect from DNA, RNA, and enzymes throughout the entire universe. Many atheists do not take issue with this. They argue against calling that cause "God," and the effect "God's creation." Richard Dawkins states, "The universe we observe has precisely the properties we should expect if there is, at bottom, no design, no purpose, no evil and no good, nothing but blind, pitiless indifference."[4] If he is correct, this is a hell of a universe to believe in! Yet, as William James said, we do not just "tolerate the material," or as Colm Tóibín put it, "I find the idea of extinction, personally, to be deeply strange and unimaginable and not something one faces with equanimity."[5]

Many atheists hold that creation is the outcome of random chance. This needs careful unpacking, because believing in randomness is akin to an act of faith. In fact, the leap of faith into randomness is a greater act of faith than our belief in a higher intelligence—God—as the primary ground of creation, for if one single and central element on earth or in the universe were not in place as it is, we would not exist as we do; we would not be here as we are. It is difficult to believe that the complexity and balance in creation—from the solar systems to the unbelievable structure of a cell—are a result of random chance. In 2007, Pope Benedict said, "The question is not to either make a decision for a creationism that fundamentally excludes science, or for an evolutionary theory that covers over its own gaps and does not want to see the questions that must be assigned to philosophy and lead beyond the realms of science. We need both."[6]

And while we are looking at the complexity and synchronicity of creation as a case for God, it is worth reflecting on the famous English naturalist and broadcaster Sir David Attenborough and his often quoted argument against belief in a good God from 2005:

> When Creationists talk about God creating every individual species as a separate act, they always instance hummingbirds, or orchids, sunflowers, and beautiful things. But I tend to think instead of a parasitic worm that is boring through the eye of a boy sitting on the bank of a river in West Africa, [a worm] that's going to make him blind. And [I ask them], "Are you telling me that the God you believe in, who you also say is an all-merciful God, who cares for each one of us individually, are you saying that God created this worm that can live in no other way than in an innocent child's eyeball? Because that doesn't seem to me to coincide with a God who's full of mercy."[7]

Given that I am not a creationist, and nor is the Catholic Church to which I belong, I have no problem believing in a loving and good God as the first cause of our evolutionary biology that over billions of years has seen glorious manifestations such as orchids and sunflowers, as well as gross corruptions and naturally occurring dysfunction like the parasitic worm, Onchocerca volvulus. I do not need God to be involved in every good or bad detail of the created order to affirm God's existence and care. Rather than disbelieving the existence of God because of a destructive worm, the challenge for humanity is to care enough about a blind boy on a river bank in Africa, and his 37 million cosufferers, to attend to the poverty and powerlessness that gives rise to plagues of infections like this one, to work to eradicate the parasite that we have known about since 1874, and to fund a campaign giving the best known treatment we have right now: moxidectin, ivermectin, and doxycycline. That would be a sign of God's mercy active in the world.

Finally, while many of us enjoy looking to science to answer satisfactorily how we are here and from where we came, science cannot answer why we are here, why life matters, whether our life is worth anything at all, and where we are headed. Some atheists argue that the "why question" is a stupid one to ask, but humans have been asking it for thousands of years. I want it answered, and science is unable to do it. I do not want to be told that life is meaningless. Faith tells the opposite story. Indeed, our belief tells us where we came from, why we are here, where we are going, and why and how we should live the best and most generous life here and now.

RELIGIOUS EXPERIENCE

A recurring element in the belief/unbelief debate is the centrality of religious experience. Some atheists claim that our religious experience leads one to believe in "imaginary friends," and helps us bolster a fragile sense of who we are and why we are here, that faith is a coping mechanism for those who need a crutch to get through life.

We know there is a vocal group of atheists who dismiss all religious experiences and any belief in God as manifestations or symptoms of a psychiatric disorder: "belief pathology."[8] Many of them claim that it is irrational to believe in anything other than that which a scientific method cannot experiment upon, test, evaluate, prove or disprove, and provide empirical proof for or against.

There are three responses to these challenges. The first is that while it is contested in some circles, many accept that there are different types of knowledge: the traditional intelligence quotient or IQ, emotional intelligence, social intelligence, and the even more recent and more contested spiritual intelligence, which attends to compassion and creativity, self-awareness and self-esteem, and flexibility and gratitude. So there is more than one way of knowing things.

The second response is that there are many human experiences that we are unable to "scientifically" test but in which we believe and trust. The best example, of course, is love, especially sacrificial love, where a believer or nonbeliever will give everything, even his or her life, for something or someone else. Some atheists intensely dislike this example, because they claim that computerized tomography (CT scans) and neurotransmitters can chart the effects of love, at least in its chemical and electrical interactive effects in the brain. Of course, the same argument can be made of every emotion. It is just that the experience of love can be totally irrational: what we love, who we love, how we love, and why we love. Love and its effects can be observed, but testing, evaluating, proving, or disproving love as an experience tests the limits of empirical knowledge.

The same case applies to forgiveness, beauty, and conscience. We know these primal human experiences to be real, powerful, and determinative. We rationally know about these realities in our life because we have experienced them. On the same basis, some of us know the reality of God because we have encountered God's love. Indeed, for Christians, religious experience is pivotal to our faith. Rather than speak about this in the abstract, let me share my own experience.

Coming from a very devout Irish Catholic Australian family, we are tribal. Growing up, my life revolved around my large extended and smaller immediate family and the local Catholic Church. I went to Catholic elementary, intermediate, and high school. My uncle was a priest and many relatives were nuns. Despite my education extending through the rebellious 1970s, I never questioned God or the prerogatives of the Church. I was a proud Catholic, but my relationship was primarily to the tribe—to the Church—not to God. At the age of fifteen, that was soon to change.

The day was toward the end of 1978, when five young Catholics walked into my high school religious education class: Peter, Judy, Maree, Vince, and Peter. They were all older than me, between eighteen and twenty-two, and I knew some of them. As soon as they started speaking, I was captivated. They began by saying they had sat where we were sitting. They identified with us as being ordinary young Catholics searching for meaning and purpose. And then they told us how they went on a retreat that changed their lives. It had been put together by a man who was to become a mentor and friend, Fr. Ray O'Leary. The entire retreat was based on the pivotal question in Mark's Gospel: "Who do you say that I am?"

The five young evangelists in my classroom consequently reported having a deep encounter with God and an experience of their faith in Christ.

I had never heard any Catholic—let alone a young adult— talk like this. Not only was their faith unashamedly public, they were palpably, infectiously happy. I knew these people. I could not dismiss them as Jesus freaks or screwballs. They lived up the street from me, and indeed, two of the four men had sat in the room where we were sitting only five years earlier. They were happy. I remember thinking that I had never seen any demonstrably happy Catholics talk about their faith like this. I was hooked.

While making this retreat, we were challenged about our faith—about Christ. We were reassured that God is loving, forgiving, and merciful. It was like I was hearing this for the first time, and it gave me hope and confidence.

There were extended periods of silence, and wonderful prayer sessions, which culminated in a long and life-changing celebration of the Eucharist, after which we were asked if we chose Christ or not. We had a very discreet and Catholic version of an altar call, where, if we chose to step out in faith, we were prayed over. There was no pressure either way. We were explicitly told that we were free to say yes or no, but in saying yes, along with scores of others, I had a religious experience, a flooding of the heart. In fact, I would not be writing this book if it were not for that retreat.

Somewhere in having a religious experience, I went from being a member of the tribe, to understanding why the tribe exists. I had an encounter with the presence of God.

Atheists often counter personal religious experience with two objections. First, it's personal and so unverifiable. To an extent, this is true because, generally, religious experiences have the status of private revelations, offering nothing significant for the wider group. Catholicism, for example, is very slow to endorse the experiences, per se, of mystics. However, it is incorrect to say that the experience is entirely beyond verification, because in almost every case, the experience causes a change in the person's life, almost always for the better. This is entirely observable. Sometimes these changes are dramatic, sometimes less so, but the change is verifiable. Exactly the same argument can be made about love. Sadly, there are some people who have not or cannot experience love, or who have encountered such evil that love for them is an idea or concept that they only hear about from the experience of another person. However, that does not mean that love does not exist, but rather that they have not had or do not want to have this encounter.

The second objection made in regard to religious experiences is that they lack crosscultural and multifaith dimensions, and that, because people have different experiences of God, God cannot be one and the same. Therefore, all personal appeals to God are false. This is a category problem. William James, an agnostic, observed that there are four elements to all mystical traditions: ineffability (the experience was often indescribable); noetic metaphysics (the experience revealed something important to the person); transience (the experience did not last and could not be summoned at call); passivity (a sense of being taken over).[9] So while there may be individual differences, there is common ground.

Furthermore and much more importantly, the Islamicist Daniel Madigan is correct in observing that, while there are crosscultural manifestations of mysticism, study of these elements alone ignores that mysticism is "mediated for us by a community and situated firmly within that community's tradition of belief." Madigan does not dismiss the reality of mystical experience or its social and religious importance, but argues that it is "firstly an experience of oneself...assenting to or achieving insight into and finally giving oneself over to the vision of reality proffered by a community that lives by that vision."

Madigan argues that mystical experience is "not so much a direct experience of God as an experience of believing." He concludes, "If religious experience appears to be a phenomenon common to all traditions, we cannot claim that it is because a single absolute or ultimate is clearly at work in them all. What gives these diverse experiences a tantalizing commonality amid all their differences is the fact that they are all instances of human persons being drawn into communal vision or hypothesis about reality."[10]

It is entirely acceptable to appeal to a personal religious experience when understood as that being mediated by one's belief, time, space, language, and culture.

If religious experience is irrational, then so are many other fundamental human encounters that give life purpose, meaning, dignity, and beauty. Consequently, appeals to all experiences would be irrational, and should not be trusted. We do not accept this in regard to other encounters like justice, truth, beauty, and goodness. Religious experience falls into the same category and builds on a similar way of proceeding.

Aggressive atheists need to be careful that their arguments are not built on the irrationality of self-importance, moral superiority, and its inherent intolerance. Christianity has been there, done that, regrets it, and lives with its consequences. The present attitude of some atheists could be colloquially expressed as this: "If only the poor, dumb religious people of the world were smarter and brighter, then they would throw off the yoke of religion." This is a form of social colonialism, which, if applied to other issues and contexts, would rightly be judged to be objectionable. Sadly, I am more than aware that some uncharitable believers offer a reverse variation on a similar theme to our nonbelieving friends—both positions are to be judged wanting. For as Terry Kelly states, "The importance of religion in the life of humanity stands: resilient throughout history; its deep appeal to the human psyche; its capacity to provide a guiding sense of ethics and morals; and its validation of mystical experiences of the 'other' that defy everyday explanations."[11]

Christian faith will not be judged by what we say as much as by what we do. As St. Francis of Assisi is reputed to have said, "Preach always and everywhere and if you must, use words." Imagine if all of the 2.3 billion Christians actually lived the faith, hope, and love we profess every day. That action alone might be enough evidence upon which to base a judgment that belief is an irresistible force for good.

The best response to any aggressive atheist is not only to point out patiently the coherence in believing in something bigger than the here and now—in something more than what we can feel, touch, and see—but also to live what we believe, practice what we preach, and to do it with love and joy. Some people may never like the message, but if it has a good effect on our lives and makes the world a better place, then that may be compelling evidence. We all know that when ideological fanatics use religion for their political ends, and when the worst criminal behaviors of a very few believers toward the most vulnerable members of society easily provide good reasons not to believe in any religion or God, then, with charity, we also need to ask what the world would be like without the best of religion.

BL. OSCAR ROMERO (1917–1980)

If ever there was someone who provides a clear example of how religious experience can transform our lives, Oscar Romero is the person.

When he was appointed archbishop of San Salvador in early 1977, Oscar Romero was a surprise choice. He was a bookish and quiet man. El Salvador was in upheaval, with a growing public defiance of the repressive military government. The junta considered Romeo a safe appointment. Then three separate events changed his life. The first happened within weeks of him being appointed archbishop. A Jesuit priest he knew and admired for his faith and work with the poor, Fr. Rutilio Grande, was killed by the military for his defense of the rights of workers and farming peasants. An old man and a young boy were also shot. The people asked Romero whether he would stand with them as Fr. Grande had done. He did. It changed his life.

The second event came the following year when three of his fellow bishops put out a letter condemning the popular people's movement as Marxist, and therefore hostile to Christianity. Romero rejected his brother bishops' claims and saw the movement as the people demanding what they had every right to have. Romero was now on a collision course with some leaders within both the Church and the state.

The third event came on January 22, 1979, when the largest political gathering ever held in El Salvador was organized. As the unarmed crowd began to pour into the Cathedral Square, the military police opened fire, killing twenty-one people and wounding

120 men, women, and children. From then on, Romero's defense of the poor and his advocacy for their dignity and rights became stronger and more international. Romero said on public radio, "I want to make a special appeal to soldiers, national guardsmen and policemen: each of you is one of us. The peasants you kill are your own brothers and sisters. When you hear a man telling you to kill, remember God's words, 'thou shalt not kill.' No soldier is obliged to obey a law contrary to the law of God. In the name of God, in the name of our tormented people, I beseech you, I implore you; in the name of God I command you to stop the repression."[12] In March, 1980, while presiding at the Eucharist, he was shot to death.

The first people honored by the earliest Christians, the first saints, were the martyrs, those who gave their lives for the faith. Our faith is built upon their witness. The word *martyr* comes from the Greek word for "witness." In fact, All Saints Day, celebrated throughout the church on November 1, has its roots in the early Church's "Martyrs Day," attested to by a hymn written in AD 359 by St. Ephraim. The name was changed to All Saints Day in the seventh century. There are three categories on the basis of which a person can be declared a saint: as a martyr, a mystic, or by their "heroic virtue." These days, most saints fall into this last group. Although Oscar Romero has not yet been canonized a saint, his cause is back on track, and many consider him a modern martyr.

The aspect of Romero's life that I find so challenging is his conversion, not to Christianity, but to the radical call of the gospel to have a faith that does justice, to the needs and rights of the poor. This process has a name. It's called "conscientization," where, as we become exposed to a new idea or a situation, we become more disposed to a new way of thinking or to the plight of the people about whom we are learning. Romero's life is a study in the process of conscientization. He was the least likely social justice reformer, but his experiences, his reflections on those experiences in the light of Jesus' teaching and example, and his relationships led him to be transformed.

Romero wanted a quiet life, away from the concerns of social inequality and human rights, a life that focused on esoteric questions of philosophical meaning. Through the process of his conscientization, he realized that the gospel calls Christians to work for the reign of Christ here on earth, not just in heaven. He saw that this reign has social and political dimensions, whereby the dignity and needs of the poor and the most vulnerable must be protected, nurtured, and respected. He learned that, when the poor have no one to fight for their God-given rights, the Church must be their voice, constructively working for a more just society and reconciling enemies. Romero became the embodiment of what the Church has called its preferential love of the poor, where we exclude no one, but just as Jesus did, we go to the margins of society and make sure everyone has a share in the good things of the earth: food, housing, education, health, and security.

Prophets and martyrs are often linked. They are put to death because they cannot live any other way. Such is the liberty of spirit, thirst for justice, and witness to truth they embody: they threaten the social and religious leaders of their time and place so much that they have to be silenced. This was exactly what happened to Romero. He did not go looking for death; it came to him.

We know from eyewitness accounts that the moment Romero was shot was during the Preparation of the Gifts at Mass. It was an extraordinary moment to die. In the Eucharist, Christians don't just remember how Jesus lived, died, and rose for them, but that his saving actions are present to us right here and now. We believe this foreshadows what all good and faithful people will enjoy in the banquet of heaven. In a sense, Romero's life was a preparation for the final, simple, but profound gifts he would offer his own people in Christ's name: courage, sacrificial love, and his own life.

We know that just like Jesus, Oscar Romero's death was not in vain. He thought he might have to pay the ultimate price: "If they kill me, I shall arise in the Salvadoran people." And that is exactly what happened. Romero's death, along with the work of many other campaigners for social justice, focused national and international attention on the military junta and it was ousted from power by 1982.

Let's conclude with a prayer inspired by Romero:

Nothing we do is complete, which is a way of saying
that the Kingdom always lies beyond us.
No statement says all that could be said.
No prayer fully expresses our faith.

No confession brings perfection.
No pastoral visit brings wholeness.
No program accomplishes the Church's mission.
No set of goals and objectives includes everything.
This is what we are about....
We cannot do everything, and there is a sense of
    liberation in realizing that.
This enables us to do something, and to do it very well.
It may be incomplete, but it is a beginning, a step along
    the way,
an opportunity for the Lord's grace to enter and do the
    rest.
We may never see the end results, but that is the
    difference
between the master builder and the worker.
We are workers, not master builders; ministers, not
    messiahs.
We are prophets of a future not our own.[13]

PART II

CHALLENGES TO
FAITH

4.

RELIGION AND WAR

Every week of my life, I have at least one conversation with believers and nonbelievers alike about challenges of faith in the contemporary world. Some of the issues people raise have seen them formally or informally depart from any identification or participation in Christianity.

With the litany of wars that have been, or are, seemingly waged in the name of God(s) throughout history, the notion that religion is the primary cause of conflict in the world can easily be asserted. I don't want to let my coreligionists off the hook for the criminal acts and suffering they have perpetrated upon our sisters and brothers, but any careful analysis bears out that religion has not been the primary cause of most wars.

Certainly, religion has had and does have a role to play in the justification of war, and some shocking deeds have been done and are done in the name of God. However, Meic Pearse presents a more intelligent analysis of the causes of war in *The Gods of War: Is Religion the Primary Cause of Violent Conflict?* Here, as well as in the highly respected *Encyclopedia of Wars*, we find, tragically, that there have been 1,763 official wars in all recorded human history. Meic Pearse shows that believers have been responsible for sixty-eight religious wars.[1]

As far as Christianity is concerned, while we hold the theory of a just war, there should not have been any war conducted simply for religious ends. To justify their murderous behavior, leaders, including religious leaders, have evoked the greatest appeal to the highest authority they can—God.

Pearse shows that the vast majority of the world's wars happen because of greed for land or resources, political power, and conflict over cultural, tribal, national, and social issues.

These days, it is tragic and wrong that some Islamists proclaim their deadly acts of terrorism as "holy wars." In the aftermath of 9/11, the world's leading mainstream Islamic leaders condemned those attacks and have subsequently condemned bin Laden, Al Qaeda, and other Islamist terrorist groups as the equivalent of war criminals whose desires do not represent Muslims and whose actions are incompatible with Islam. There are approximately 1.6 billion Muslims in the world, the vast majority of whom live by the often-quoted teaching in the Qur'an: "If any one slew a person...it would be as if he slew the whole people: and if any one saved a life, it would be as if he saved the life of the whole people" (Surat Al-Mā'idah, 5:32).

Nor do I want to pretend that all is fine with Islam.

We need to be upfront but clear about the present issues regarding Islam. The distinguished journalist Fareed Zakaria, born into an Islamic family, neatly sums up the grave issues:

> But let's be honest. Islam has a problem today. The places that have trouble accommodating themselves to the modern world are disproportionately Muslim. In 2013, of the top 10 groups that perpetrated terrorist attacks, seven were Muslim. Of the top 10 countries where terrorist attacks took place, seven were Muslim-majority. The Pew Research Center rates countries on the level of restrictions that governments impose on the free exercise of religion. Of the 24 most restrictive countries, 19 are Muslim-majority. Of the 21 countries that have laws against apostasy, all have Muslim majorities. There is a cancer of extremism within Islam today. A small minority of Muslims celebrates violence and intolerance and harbors deeply reactionary attitudes toward women and minorities. While some confront these extremists, not enough do so, and the protests are not loud enough. How many mass rallies have been

held against the Islamic State (also known as ISIS) in the Arab world today?[2]

The reality is that religion, as one among many tools, has been and is sometimes used in political, social, and ethnic wars, in the false search for social and political uniformity and colonial dominance. Furthermore, apart from war, and even more tragically, religion has mounted its own persecutions.

Let's not run away from the despicable fallout from the 595-year reign of the "inquisitors of heretical depravity." It is impossible to know how many people were actually killed in this period by these theological tyrants, but most reputable scholars on the Inquisition conclude that it was somewhere between three and five thousand people. Not one person should have been murdered for who they were (homosexuals), for what they did (notorious sinners and so-called witches), or for what they believed (atheists, Jews, and Muslims). Having now formally apologized for the Inquisition (easy in hindsight), to my knowledge the Catholic Church has not sanctioned the death of anyone since 1826, which is more than we can say for most other nations or states.

Humanity does not need religion to be murderous. A horrible statistic to know is that the atheistic regimes of the Soviet Union, Communist China, the Nazis, Pol Pot, and other nationalist regimes accounted for 1.2 billion deaths in the twentieth century. Some atheists object to believers making such a claim. For example, Sam Harris states,

> People of faith often claim that the crimes of Hitler, Stalin, Mao and Pol Pot were the inevitable product of unbelief. The problem is that they are too much like religions. Such regimes are dogmatic to the core and generally give rise to personality cults that are indistinguishable from cults of religious hero worship....There is no society in human history that ever suffered because its people became too reasonable.[3]

That these murderous regimes and their evil output were inevitable products of their unbelief is unconvincing. However, these regimes were atheistic in word and deed, and mounted the largest-scale and most systematic murder of innocents the world has ever known. Clifford Geertz once famously defined religion as "a system of symbols, which acts to establish powerful, pervasive, and long-lasting moods and motivations in men [*sic*] by formulating conceptions of a general order of existence and clothing these conceptions with such an aura of factuality that the moods and motivations seem uniquely realistic."[4] Given this, we can see some validity in Harris's argument in regard to the symbolic presentations of communism, fascism, and Nazism, but the same could also be applied to some families, sporting clubs, and social institutions that have elaborate quasireligious rituals. Just borrowing and adapting religious-style myths and rituals does not lead to murderous behavior by a state or group; nor does it mean that religions inevitably murder because of their myths and rituals. Harris seems to be arguing that if the world had his brand of atheism—against those other murderous brands—we would not have any murder.

The sad reality is that in human conflict, especially when it involves greed for land or resources, political power, and conflict over cultural, tribal, national, and social issues, religion is one of the many things used to uphold the rightness of the claim and the justification for war.

Despite what some atheists say, religions change, develop, and evolve. The believers interpret their sacred texts in the light of tools at their disposal in order to understand their own history: they discern the essentials of their faith from those texts that refer to a time and period that has passed, and they take into account the contemporary setting in living the faith. All religions have some way to go in this regard, but the intelligent and common-sense majority should not be summarily condemned along with the distorted ideology that can emerge from the most unwell, ignorant, or criminal religious minority.

Does anyone truly believe that if you had no religion at all, we would have no wars? So, it is simply not true to say that Christianity or religion has been the cause and effect of most wars in the world.

5.

FAITH, RELIGION, AND CHILD SEXUAL ABUSE

Over the past twenty years, I cannot recall a conversation about the validity of religion where this issue has not been raised. This has a personal edge for me. Since being ordained in 1993, I have seriously questioned my vocation on three occasions, and each time the questioning emerged out of revelations about the crimes of clergy against minors and the cover-up of those crimes by Church officials.

There is no question that this criminal behavior has been one of the greatest moments of evil, both in the abuse, itself, and in its cover-up. Having established the Pontifical Commission for the Protection of Minors to deal with clerical sex abuse, Pope Francis stated, "We must go ahead with zero tolerance. A priest who has sex with a child betrays God. A priest needs to lead children to sanctity, and children trust him. But instead he abuses them, and this is terrible."[5]

Then, in his meeting with survivors of clerical abuse on Monday, July 7, 2014, he said even more clearly,

> There is no place in the Church's ministry for those who commit these abuses, and I commit myself not to tolerate harm done to a minor by any individual, whether a cleric or not. All bishops must carry out their pastoral ministry with the utmost care in order to help foster the

protection of minors, and they will be held accountable....I ask (your) support so as to help me ensure
that we develop better policies and procedures in the
universal Church for the protection of minors and for
the training of church personnel in implementing those
policies and procedures. We need to do everything in
our power to ensure that these sins have no place in the
Church....(May God) give us the grace to be ashamed.[6]

For those of us who have met survivors of clerical sexual
abuse of minors, and the secondary victims, their families, we
know that no apology can ever repair the damage, no amount of
compensation can give someone back their innocence and childhood, and no act of reparation or penance can ever adequately
express the shame and sorrow of what all of us feel over what a
very few clergy have done.

That said, along with other Catholics, I hope, first, that all
Church officials against whom credible allegations of child abuse
have been upheld will be dismissed from the priesthood and religious life. No matter when it was committed, the sexual abuse of
a child nullifies any commitment to the priesthood or belonging
to a religious order. It is, for many believers, the line in the sand.
Christian forgiveness starts with holding people accountable for
what they have done, and it has consequences. While no one is
beyond God's mercy and forgiveness, some actions by a very few
Church officials prevent them from continuing to be such leaders.

Second, if the survivor wishes to go to the police, the Church
should support them in their decision, be transparent in the legal
process, and hand over the alleged perpetrator for secular legal investigation. Third, if the survivor does not wish to pursue a legal remedy, the Church needs to establish the truth of their claims through
an independent conciliation, arbitration, and compensation process. Fourth, officials who have covered up these crimes should
be subjected to civil and ecclesiastical penalties. Finally, if the
pursuit of justice means that the Church needs to sell property
and liquidate assets to settle just claims with survivors, then the
Church should recognize that people always matter more than
land and buildings. Though no cash can ever repair the damage,

it is one indication of the seriousness of action in the face of our new-found rhetoric.

There are, however, four other related issues in this conversation. First, without justifying one case, clergy are not the only people to have abused a child and Church officials are not the only ones to cover it up. In every OECD country, the most common place for a child to be abused is in the family home by a person known to the family. In most of these countries, that rate has hovered around 83 percent of all cases for over two decades. While it is true that religious officials who preach social and personal morality should be held to a higher standard than most, it would be a rare individual who would argue that expectations in regard to a child's family should be any less than in religious organizations. Because we know that prosecution rates of family abusers do not follow anything like these consistent statistics, then we can conclude that a tremendous number of families also know about covering up this crime.

Second, credibility demands that we are consistent on the question of child sexual abuse and child protection, so, no matter when it was committed, child sexual abuse in a family must be reported to the police and the alleged perpetrator handed over for investigation. If the victim does not wish to pursue a legal remedy, there must be an independent conciliation, arbitration, and compensation process for them to access. The family may need to come to a just settlement with the victim. Any member of the family who has covered up these crimes should also be subjected to civil penalties as well.

It is perfectly understandable why it is easier for some people to get angry with churches in regard to sexual abuse of children. However, it is fair to acknowledge that, seeing this crime as a moral failure—one that could be changed when challenged—it did not have to be reported to the police even though laws specifically forbidding child sexual abuse emerged in most OECD countries in the 1960s and 1970s (yes, incredibly, they are that late). Tragically and tellingly, child sexual abuse can be found wherever there is access, power, and pathology. To be ruthlessly consistent, which I assume all people of good will want to be in regard to child protection issues, we should soon see active and retired government officials, school leaders, sporting coaches and college presidents, retired and serving officers in the defense forces, Scouts, officials of every other major Christian denomination, and other religious groups be equally scrutinized, charged, and convicted for the crimes and the cover-up of the crimes.

Third, while I long to see a change to the discipline of mandatory celibacy for Catholic diocesan priests, it should not be because of child sexual abuse. There can be little doubt that in some cases celibacy has been a disaster in the psycho-sexual maturity of some individuals, and most studies do find that celibate priests commit abuse at a higher rate than the population as a whole, and in comparison to married men. However, the same studies also point to other factors like access and power.

From personal experience, celibacy also enshrines a class or caste system in the Catholic Church that can be secretive, unaccountable, unassailable, and doesn't have to answer to secular community standards, valuations, and expectations. As in most things, celibacy can be a life-giving gift of oneself for the betterment of humanity, but it can also be a force for personal and communal destruction. Therefore, I welcome a change in the discipline of celibacy for diocesan priests, but prefer that it not be in response to child protection issues because that will not solve the problem.

Finally, it is often claimed that the place where clergy are most protected is in the Catholic confessional. Ever since Hitchcock's 1953 film, *I Confess*, the public has seen this moment as potentially sinister. Priests break the "seal of confession" if the identity of the penitent is exposed in any way, but priests are able to talk about "cases" in exactly the same way lawyers or doctors can do so. More generally, I have never heard the confession of anyone admitting to child sexual abuse. I have asked at least a hundred other priests of varying ages if they ever heard the confession of a pedophile priest. None have and I believe them. So, while it is possible, and may even seem accommodating for the Church to give them a veil of secrecy in the confessional, it would be extremely rare for a child abuser who needs silence to do his evil actions to take the risk of telling anyone about what he has done. We also know that pedophiles lead psychologically compartmentalized lives. So, while the general public thinks that child-abusing priests, for example, must need to repent of their crimes to function, psychological and family studies tell us that perpetrators do not process these actions in the same way the rest of us do and that, as difficult as it is for anyone of us to accept, these criminals can abuse children and carry on with their daily lives as though no crime has been committed.

To my knowledge, there are only two vocations whose professional disclosures are presently protected by the courts: lawyers and priests. Doctors used to be, but now they must mandatorily report any child sexual abuse. (I have often wondered how psychiatrists cope with that one.) However, the nature of the conversations of lawyers and priests has been recognized as having qualities that the law deems should be protected, and that are related.

If a person is to be defended, the lawyer needs to know the truth, even if some of the truth they hear is criminal. They need the whole story. If a penitent is to repent, then he or she needs to be able to tell the truth. The priest should hear the whole story. If we now make the priest liable for what they hear in confession, then I assume we could also make lawyers liable for what they hear from clients in conference. No exceptions.

In any case, in the extremely unlikely event that someone came to me to confess the sin of child sexual abuse, it does not mean that they are automatically forgiven by God or the Church. To fulfill all the obligations of the sacrament, they have to be sorry for their sins, have a sincere purpose to amend their lives (stop the crimes), and as an expression of this, they must do their penance. I would make absolution contingent on that penitence and me notifying the police immediately—right there and then. No penance, no absolution. This is, clearly, not foolproof and, more seriously, it is not right in the face of the crime, but I could not imagine anyone, who has no desire to take responsibility for what they had done to their victims, actually and genuinely coming to the sacrament of penance, confessing this egregious sin, and allowing me to accompany them to the authorities.

For consistency, I often wonder if those who are interested in the confessional seal would also want priests to report other illegal behavior we may hear such as drug use; any type of theft; any physical or sexual abuse of adults—especially rape in marriage; some forms of pornography; avoidance of taxation; software piracy; hastening death or assisting a suicide; and the failure of anyone to report a crime to the police. It was not long ago that it would have also meant reporting a woman who had an abortion. Given the current civil law in some countries, it would also mean that Catholic priests would have to report adultery and homosexuality to the police. Some of our detractors want to spend a lot of time and energy on this issue in regard to child sexual abuse in the Church, and while it is an interesting conversation to have, the actual experience of priests in the confessional bears out the truth of the old ethical line: extreme cases don't prove principles.

That said, I think the sexual abuse of children is a crisis for all the churches. It is a make-or-break moment for many people concerning belief, unbelief, membership, and belonging and even whether the churches can be trusted at all, about anything. The stakes are presently very high. No one who cares about the Church can minimize the gravity of the crisis anymore.

THE WITNESS TO TRUTH

In this crisis, there are two things that inspire me about survivors and their families, to whom are owed the first claim of our care and attention. The first is that they kept telling the truth when no one wanted to hear it. This often started in their families who were sometimes hostile and disbelieving because they, like many of us, could not believe that a particular priest or brother would be capable of such a heinous act. Then the person or the family encountered an institution who wanted to deny the truth and protect the assets. As we now know, the Catholic Church was not on its own in this regard, just an appalling "exhibit A" of what not to do. The armed forces, government departments, especially those who presided over state-run homes for children, every other Christian denomination, Islam, Judaism, and the Scouting Movement, were all equally self-protective. Leaders often thought that if they ignored the case, which was in fact presented by a very vulnerable and courageous person, it might go away; they argued that the cases were isolated, and that the good name of the institution should be protected above all. Well, look at the so-called good name of some of these institutions now. True repentance and reconciliation starts with telling the truth, no matter how painful it is to say or hear it. Healing begins with being believed. The rage and courage of survivors and their families, the priests who supported them against the odds, the journalists who reported their stories, the police who began investigating, and the politicians who took on institutional power no matter what—these people inspire me to do what can now be done to make amends, to bring healing where possible, and to attend to the institutional root causes that saw the crimes, criminals, and cover-ups thrive.

Furthermore, I do not want to be one of those priests who presume that simply telling the truth and being believed is enough. In the traditional culture of indigenous Australians, when an offense has been committed, the community must do "payback." If the crime is significant, the restitution involves the perpetrator, or the family, spilling blood. In Western countries, the equivalent of spilling blood is through a monetary settlement. It can hurt the individual or the family or the institution. It can be necessary as a way of saying that we are serious about healing and our sincere purpose is amendment. I expect we will be a smaller, poorer church in the years to come, but rightly so!

The second way survivors inspire me is that they have survived. I know of six victims of sexual abuse by Church personnel who have committed suicide. I did the funerals of two of them. They are among the saddest services I have ever done. The justified anger toward the Church is felt and expressed. However, funerals are for the living not for the dead, and these families knew that the Church is greater than the criminal abuser, and that a church service would help them say goodbye and grieve more than any other alternative.

When a victim of clergy sexual abuse suicides, the one question we are not left with is "Why?" We know why. His or her childhood was robbed from him or her. Innocence was taken away. He or she was left feeling guilty and ashamed. The consequence of this trauma is often chronic depression. Many victims are also very good at covering it up, presenting well and even overachieving. It's only in retrospect that many of the person's family or friends remember a conversation, a moment, or an event where they glimpse the shadow—but it is difficult to know its depth. Depression thrives in hidden places, in silence. In either case, sometimes the shadow takes over, or the person we know to have a heart of gold, be loving, fun, talented, and compassionate, loses the battle with the heart of darkness.

The research we have from people who attempt suicide and live says that they did not want to die; they wanted the pain to stop. Despite the love and support and the drugs and therapy, the pain inflicted by a trusted churchman becomes too much to bear. They do not rationally choose death; they become powerless in the face of the pain, and can no longer live with it.

Other survivors inspire me because at some stage they share the trauma of what happened to them and get the help they need and deserve. Some have a very public battle with depression or other mental illnesses for the rest of their lives, but their families and friends hang in there with them. Others take the trauma and demand justice. They speak for the living, who cannot find their voice, and they speak for the dead. We need them.

6.

IS THE BIBLE FACT OR FICTION?

When I began studying for the priesthood, we were told that at some stage in our formation we would have to spend a year addressing our personal issues professionally with a psychiatrist so that, potentially, we would not lump them on to others in the future. Many of my contemporaries resented this requirement as an imposition. I am not sure what it says about me; I loved it! Someone was going to be paid to listen to me each week for a whole year. Mind you, my psychiatrist went to sleep on me four times that year. That's how exciting my psyche was. In fact, I thought I should invent some stories just to keep my shrink awake!

Regardless, of all the wonderful observations this psychiatrist made to me that year, among his best was, "I know when someone has moved from adolescence to adulthood because they are not emotionally all or nothing." He gave me an example of a fifteen-year-old girl who asks her parents for permission to go to a local dance. "We would be delighted for that, darling," says Dad, "but Mom and I want you home by 10:30 p.m." With a big pout, his adolescent daughter replies, "Well, I'm not going then. If I can't stay out until midnight like everyone else, then I won't go." She doesn't go. For most adolescents, life is reduced to all or nothing, black or white, it's true or false. I know a good many fifty-year-olds who are only fifteen years of age emotionally.

This advice is helpful in approaching the Bible. Many young and not-so-young adults, believers and unbelievers alike, want the Bible to be either all true or all false. This position is theologically adolescent. The Bible is, literally, a library of books of varying relevance, importance, and application. Though we can enter into its riches on many levels, to get the most out of it, we need to pay careful attention to it as a literary text: its history, the time and circumstance of its writing, the community who produced it, the way it reflects its culture, and the larger religious messages that emerge from it. Any one part of a particular book, and any one book within the Bible, needs to be read against the wider message of the Bible as a whole. This is especially true for Christians as we read parts of the Old Testament.

Until the late nineteenth century, the vast majority of Christians read the Bible literally. Even though it sometimes contradicted itself, it was the word of God, and so every detail of it had to be factually true. This position always had problems. For instance, there is not just one Creation story—the famous seven-day version in Genesis 1. In Genesis 2, we have another Creation story where we are not told how long Creation took, but it seems to happen very quickly, and it occurs in a completely different order from Genesis 1. In this second Creation account, the garden is not perfect but a place of work, and some spaces in it are already dangerous and off-limits. Lesser known Creation stories come later in Psalm 104 and Job 38, where God just places the earth on its axis on the sea. Then in Psalm 74, we are told that God creates the order of the world by first slaying the chaos created by sea monsters. The Bible's cosmology looks like this:

- the earth was flat, motionless, and sitting serenely at the center of a simple three-layered universe with heaven above and hell below;
- the sun, moon, stars, and other heavenly bodies circled a stationary earth;
- the flat earth rested on pillars;
- the moon emitted light;
- the universe is composed of water, and
- rain occurred when God opened up windows in the sky.

If we are looking for science here, we are in trouble. It cannot all be factual, and none of it is. It is the best a prescientific people could do to explain the created order. They did their best with what they had.

For over a century, Christians have been seeking to under-stand better the Bible's theology, history, literature, culture, context, and the communities that produced each of the books in the biblical library. Though many of us were taught otherwise, by well-meaning preachers and teachers, for the last fifty years, the Catholic Church has taught that the Bible is not to be interpreted literally.

Nevertheless, we are not theologically adolescent. We are not all or nothing. The Bible is not just all right or all wrong. Bernard Lonergan, SJ, has offered a very helpful contribution to this debate. Lonergan makes a distinction between truth and fact.[7] Although the Bible contains some facts, it was not written, and nor should it be interpreted, as a book of facts. It was written as stories, historical accounts, wisdom, poetry, prophecies, letters, parables, and apocalyptic literature to evoke images, emotions, and responses to the religious truths it is expounding. So the Bible is a library of books of varying relevance and importance containing religious truths. The Catholic Church believes the Bible cannot err in revealing to us what we need to know for our salvation, notably God's saving love and mercy.

As Christians, of course, we believe that Jesus is the definitive revelation of God for the world, so we have to approach all revelation in the Old Testament through the prism of Christ. As Christians, we believe that if there is a conflict between the image of God that emerges between some parts of the Old Testament and the definitive revelation of God in Jesus Christ, then we go for Jesus. It concerns me that some people think we have a split-personality God: nasty God the Father in heaven who kills and maims and inflicts plagues upon creation; loving Jesus; and the bird-like Spirit who hovers around and abides with us still. But we do not believe this. The Father, Son, and Spirit are three personae of the one, same God. Saint John of Damascus said the Trinity was a dance, a *Pas de trois*. Saint Ignatius Loyola described it as three notes in a single chord. Saint Patrick famously used the three-leaf clover as a teaching aid to get the point across to the Irish, and St. Augustine thought the Trinity acted in unison in the same way that the combination of memory, intelligence, and will does within each of us.

Not being a Jew, I can let go of the Hebrew interpretation of the presence and action of God in various events of their history because some images are completely irreconcilable with the person and work of Christ. I can understand why Richard Dawkins could say, "The God of the Old Testament is arguably the most unpleasant character in all fiction: jealous and proud of it; a petty, unjust, unforgiving control-freak; a vindictive, bloodthirsty ethnic cleanser; a misogynistic, homophobic, racist, infanticidal, genocidal, filicidal, pestilential, megalomaniacal, sadomasochistic, capriciously malevolent bully."[8] Conveniently, what Dawkins does not say in his selective caricature is that there are many more instances in the Old Testament where God is also presented as loving, forgiving, gentle, compassionate, just, merciful, faithful, and joyous.

When it comes to Jesus, however, there is not a single moment in the New Testament when Jesus is petty, unjust, an unforgiving control freak, vindictive, a bloodthirsty ethnic cleanser; a misogynist, homophobic, racist, infanticidal, genocidal, filicidal, pestilential, megalomaniacal, sadomasochistic, or capriciously malevolent bully.

Don't turn the cleansing of the temple in John 2, for example, into a frenzy of bloody violence. In this scene, which is in all four Gospels, Jesus becomes angry at the unjust exploitation of the poor in God's name. It is only in John that we are told, in the Greek text, that with uncharacteristic anger, he "made a whip from cords," not a Roman scourge, and he sent the money changers scurrying.

In fact, Christianity has regularly let go of the Hebrew interpretation of the presence and action of God in various events of their history. It is not some new trendy Christian theology, but we have always believed that Jesus corrects as well as fulfills the Old Testament. As John records, "If you know me, you will know my Father also. From now on you do know him and have seen him.... Whoever has seen me has seen the Father....The words that I say to you I do not speak on my own; but the Father who dwells in me does his works. Believe me that I am in the Father and the Father is in me...and the word that you hear is not mine, but is from the

Father who sent me (John 14:7–24). This is why Christians inter-mittently left behind animal sacrifices, selling our children into slavery, infanticide, mandatory circumcision, killing anyone who works on the Sabbath, and declaring that pigs, camels, carnivorous birds, sea creatures without fins and scales, most insects, rodents, and reptiles were unclean and could not be eaten.

It is true that first-century Christians did not leave everything behind, some of which we now wish they had. It took Christians centuries to see the inhumanity of slavery, and this includes Pope Nicholas V's shameful 1452 decree that Catholic nations had the right to enslave non-Christians. However, it was also devout Chris-tians like William Wilberforce in 1785, and Charles Spurgeon, John Wesley, Charles Finney, Theodore Weld, George Bourne, George B. Cheever, Pope Benedict XIV in 1741, Pius VII in 1815, Daniel O'Connell and the Quaker abolitionists, Benjamin Lay, and John Woolman who, along with many great secularists in these centuries, vigorously denounced slavery and agitated for an end to this evil.

Similarly, there is no question that Christian thinking on the role and leadership of women is going through a similar and wel-come development. It is equally true that science is rightly and presently challenging the biblical presumptions behind the nature and nurture debate in regard to homosexuality. It is important to note here, again, that while Jesus has next to nothing to say about human sexuality in the Gospels, he has much to say about the dignity of all people, the command to love oneself, and of the universal call to be compassionate.

So letting go of some of the time-bound customs in the Bible is a work in progress for all Christians, informed now by the best of biblical studies, modern psychology, science, and philosophy. As "people of the Book," we are not frightened of the contempo-rary world, we use it to enable us to illuminate the central truths within the biblical library that is read in the light of the teaching of Jesus, so we can live our salvation here and now.

7.

THE HISTORICAL JESUS

There are some who argue that Jesus is a historical invention, but they are in the vast minority of opinion, scholarly or otherwise. It is true that the earliest written evidence of Jesus is found in the New Testament, which clearly has a stake in the story! Though the order is debated, the first six writings are generally agreed to be the Letter of James, dating from around AD 50, 1 Thessalonians (52–53), 2 Thessalonians (52–53), Galatians (55), 1 Corinthians (57), and 2 Corinthians (57–58). Given that Jesus most probably died in Jerusalem between AD 34 and 36, the first written material about Jesus comes sixteen to twenty-two years after he lived, probably because the first eyewitnesses to his life were dying.

We also have two other nonbiblical sources. In his *Antiquities of the Jews* (ca. AD 93), Jewish historian Josephus tells us that Jesus was crucified on the orders of Pontius Pilate. In the *Annals* (ca. AD 116), the Roman historian Tacitus also records that Pilate crucified Jesus.

Rather than citing instances of a man called Jesus, however, maybe the many references to the earliest followers of Jesus are equally telling. Explaining why Nero blamed the Christians for the fire of Rome in AD 64, Tacitus writes, "Nero fastened the guilt… on a class hated for their abominations, called Christians by the populace. Christus, from whom the name had its origin, suffered the extreme penalty during the reign of Tiberius at the hands of…Pontius Pilatus, and a most mischievous superstition, thus checked for the moment, again broke out not only in Judaea, the first source of the evil, but even in Rome" (*Annals*, 15.44).

In AD 112, Pliny the Younger wrote to Emperor Trajan about if and how he should prosecute the "great many" cases against people accused of being Christians:

> They were in the habit of meeting on a certain fixed day before it was light, when they sang in alternate verses a hymn to Christ, as to a god, and bound themselves by a solemn oath, not to any wicked deeds, but never to commit any fraud, theft or adultery, never to falsify their word, nor deny a trust when they should be called upon to deliver it up; after which it was their custom to separate, and then reassemble to partake of food—but food of an ordinary and innocent kind.[9]

There are also passing references to Jesus and Christians in the earlier writings in the Babylonian Talmud, a collection of Jewish rabbinical writings from AD 70 to 200. Lucian of Samosata, a Greek satirist, wrote in *The Death of Peregrine* (AD 165–175) that "the Christians…worship a man to this day—the distinguished personage who introduced their novel rites, and was crucified on that account….[It] was impressed on them by their original lawgiver that they are all brothers, from the moment that they are converted, and deny the gods of Greece, and worship the crucified sage, and live after his laws."[10]

However, even more striking proof comes from actions rather than words. Apart from the New Testament, where we hear about Saul murdering Stephen for his faith in Jesus, and the martyrdom of James, son of Zebedee, Josephus documents the martyrdom of James the Just. And from the documents we have from Imperial Rome, we know the Roman's first systematic, as against local, persecution of Christians began in Rome in AD 64. Therefore, about thirty-four to thirty-six years after Jesus had died, the Emperor Nero decreed that Christianity was punishable by death. Anyone who would not offer sacrifice to the Roman gods could be and was often killed by the state. Later Christians claimed that it was during this time that Peter was martyred.

A century later, in AD 164, there are Roman records of Justin Martyr and his six fellow Christians going on trial and being executed. The later reigns of Emperors Decius, Diocletian, and Galerius were especially bloody for Christians. In all of this, the earliest and later Christians were not giving their lives for a phantom, an idea, or a cause. They were giving their lives in following Jesus, the one they called the Christ.

Insofar as we can establish for certain that the then-secondary figures of the ancient world lived, we know that a man called Jesus from Nazareth lived and died in Palestine in the first part of the first century. When we move from all the historical evidence and probabilities that we can muster to the claims made about Jesus by Christians, these claims clearly fall within the ambit of faith: they cannot be scientifically proved or disproved. In any case, other examples of similar claims in other mythologies and religions show that the ancient world saw the singularity and prominence of the person through these elements within the narrative.

What we do know is that within a decade of Jesus' life, death, and resurrection, Christianity is found in nearly every major center in the eastern Roman Empire: Jerusalem, Antioch, Ephesus, Corinth, Thessalonica, Cyprus, Crete, and Rome. It spread like wildfire. Why? Whatever else happened after the death of Jesus, something so powerful was unleashed that, among others, uneducated Galilean fishermen, together with the Pharisee and Roman citizen Saul/Paul, were so emboldened by their experience of Jesus that they took on the might of the Roman Empire and, like generations after them, were prepared to pay the price of following him even to the point of death. Very few people will die for nothing; something had happened to them all.

8.

A LOVING GOD, JESUS, AND GOOD FRIDAY

There is hardly a more debated area of theology these days than what Protestants call "satisfaction theology" and Catholics call "atonement theory." Though the emphasis is different for both groups, these ideas wrestle with why Jesus died on Good Friday, and what role a loving God had in it.

First, an important aside: I have come to believe that we should be very careful about what we sing. Spiritual songs and hymns are not part of our liturgy to fill in time, to accompany a procession, or to annoy the tone-deaf who are pressed into making a noise. Hymns carry theology. We sing scriptural texts or a poetic version of a fundamental Christian truth to affirm and proclaim our faith. Setting these texts to music makes them popular and memorable. This is why they can be so powerful, important, and dangerous—think of the gospel song, "We Shall Overcome."

One verse of one hymn has more to answer for than most. "How Great Thou Art" takes its place in the top five of nearly every survey of the most-loved hymns in the English-speaking world. Written by the Swedish Lutheran, lay preacher, poet, writer, and later elected official Carl Gustav Boberg in 1885, "O Store Gud" (O great God) was translated into English by Stuart Hine. Hine was an English evangelical missionary in the Ukraine, where he learned the hymn in Russian. In 1939, he returned to England and the following year published the first version of the hymn we now call "How Great Thou Art." Its worldwide fame is attributed to Billy Graham's International Crusade in London during 1954, during which time this hymn was sung over and over as it accompanied the altar call, and was broadcast and televised to an audience of millions. And it did not hurt the hymn's fortunes that it was the Grammy Award–winning title song of Elvis Presley's 1967 hit record.

The Protestant pedigree of this hymn is important, but a little history first to try and understand why we got trapped into believing in such a bloodthirsty God. To do so we need to remember that, until the last hundred years, the entire Christian tradition read the Bible literally. This is no one's fault. In the wake of science challenging biblical ideas in the Enlightenment, the nineteenth century saw the coming together of rationalist philosophy, advances in comparative literature and languages, archaeology, and historical methods that were then applied to the texts, contexts, sources, forms, and literary styles of the books in the Bible. Furthermore, throughout the twentieth century, science was able to propose and debate coherent theories about how the earth and humanity evolved. However, this meant that previous thinking in regard to the literal truth of Genesis had to be revisited.

The traditional understanding of why Jesus died is entirely dependent on a literal reading of chapter 2 in Genesis, where humanity's original parents, Adam and Eve, offended God by eating of the fruit of the tree of knowledge, in an attempt to establish themselves as God, knowing good and evil. This triggers a series of events: loss of innocence; hiding from God; blaming each other for the action; the serpent condemned as the embodiment of evil; women suffering in childbirth; and, later, Adam and Eve expelled from Eden, the garden of paradise. The reverse side of Adam and Eve's original sin is the alienation it established between the perfect Creator and his imperfect and rebellious creatures, and his subsequent lament and anger at humanity's fall into sinfulness. Questions arise in this literal reading of Genesis. God creates humanity with the freedom to choose, and then seems angry when they exercise that choice. As represented by the serpent, evil is created by God—a very problematic proposition for a truly and fully loving being—who seems to invest the serpent with stronger powers of persuasion than he has. Having been set up for a fall in *the* fall, Adam and Eve are punished for their sin by being alienated from God, as expressed in them roaming the earth. Subsequent presentations of God's anger at our lack of fidelity may suggest that God is no better than we are—brooding and angry—since humanity was created for a situation that we did not create and that was the result of a bad choice when it was offered. Furthermore, it can be argued that God appears imperfect until the final repenting sacrifice is made, and somehow we had to do something, in Jesus and to Jesus in the crucifixion, to fulfill this need in God.

These days, we now read these chapters as the Hebrews theologizing about how evil came into the world, why human beings sin and are imperfect, and about our estrangement from God.

Once the breach between heaven and earth had begun, the rest of the Old Testament could be fairly described as God wrestling with his chosen people to bring about a healing of the breach. Israel longed and hoped and looked for the day when such a remarriage between heaven and earth could occur.

As Israel kept reflecting on how reconciliation might be effected, a central metaphor emerged from the years during which the Israelites wandered in the desert. The Messiah, the anointed one, would be the one who would bring them home. Though there are several expectations of the Messiah in the Old Testament, it was generally thought that he would restore Israel either politically, ethically, or ritually. In Isaiah 53, we hear that this Suffering Servant would also be wounded for the sins of humanity and be the offering to God as an innocent scapegoat for all, or as a spotless lamb, offered on behalf of humanity, so that through him God's reign of justice and peace would be established.

Israel adopted a transactional model to explain what must occur. Original sin was conceived as a moral and personal debt owed to God, and which needed to be repaid. Humanity was fallen, so we could not make the sacrifice and pay the debt, because no matter how well-intentioned and fully undertaken our offering might be, it would always remain imperfect. In Christian theology, it is the perfect Son who becomes the perfect man and can make the perfect sacrifice to the perfect God, and so the breach is healed, and heaven is again wedded to earth.

It is from this theology that the Protestant satisfaction theology was born by giving it a more biblical spin: God's wrath or anger was finally and totally "satisfied." Relying on a literal and even tougher stand on the role of the fall of Adam and Eve, John Calvin held that because the first parents of humanity in Genesis rebelled against God, our entire human nature was corrupted forever. There was nothing we could do about it. God was so angry with us but, in time and in his mercy, and even though we did not deserve it, he decided to save us. But because humanity could not do anything to save itself, to satisfy God's wrath at Adam and Eve and all humanity's subsequent ingratitude, the Word of God had to take our flesh, our place, and offer up the sacrifice of his own life in and through his suffering and death as atonement for our inherited and ongoing sinfulness.

Catholic theology developed a theory of atonement describing the death of Jesus, as in the pattern of the atoning sacrifices of the temple, as definitively reconciling creation to God. This has roots in the New Testament. Christian teaching that Jesus' death pays off the debt of our sin to God begins with St. Paul, who writes that "Christ Jesus, whom God put forward as a sacrifice of atonement by his blood, effective through faith" (Rom 3:24–25). And later, explicitly drawing out the parallel with Adam in an understandably literal reading of Genesis, "Therefore, just as sin came into the world through one man [Adam], and death came through sin, and so death spread to all because all have sinned....just as by the one man's disobedience the many were made sinners, so by the one man's obedience the many will be made righteous" (Rom 5:12, 19). Saint Paul argues this was the work of our redemption.

Understanding this concept of redemption holds the key to another way forward. The word *redemption* literally means "buying back." It comes from the practice in the ancient world where there were two types of slaves—those who were born or forced into slavery, usually for life, and others who paid off a debt or a crime by becoming a slave, usually for a period of time. The second type of slaves could be set free when someone else paid their debts, or the ransom their master now demanded for them was settled. They would, then, either be the slave of the purchaser, or set free completely.

Saint Paul introduced this metaphor into Christian theology to describe how we, who are enslaved by our destructive behavior, gained a liberator in Christ, who entered into a sinful world and subjected himself to its violence and death in order to set us free. At its best, the notion of Christ the Redeemer shows us that we do not have to live destructively anymore. Now claimed by the love of Christ, we are no longer slaves, but his friends; indeed, through the redeeming work of Christ, we have been welcomed into God's family and shown the path to life.

This theology was developed in the work of St. Clement of Alexandria (ca. AD 150–215) and St. Anselm of Canterbury, an eleventh-century Benedictine monk, as they wrestled with the question why God came into the world as one like us. In his famous treatise *Cur Deus Homo* (Why God became human), he developed a theory that Jesus came into the world to act as a substitute for us. We were the ones who had offended God, but rather than sacrifice us all, God sent Jesus to take our place in offering up his own life to the Father as restitution for our sins. He paid the ransom that God demanded to set us free.

For Christians, the paschal mystery—the life, death, and resurrection of Jesus—is the central paradigm around which our faith in God is constructed. However, the Word of God did not become one with us as a human being simply and only to die. If that were baldly true, then why did God spare him from the outcome of the most unjust theological story in the New Testament—Matthew's slaughter of the innocents (Matt 2:13–23)? If Jesus had been murdered by Herod at two years of age, then God could have gotten his blood sacrifice over nice and early. If all God wanted was the perfect blood offering of his only Son for the sake of appeasing his anger, why did Jesus not leave Nazareth, stir up plenty of trouble around Galilee (as he did), and then march straight into Jerusalem and offend everyone and get crucified early on? It would not have been hard. If Jesus had simply been sent "to die," then what was the reason for his hidden years and his years of public ministry? They were not for God's sake, but for ours.

There are libraries written on the stuff of the last couple of pages, but for our purposes, this wholly inadequate summary will have to do.

In its more stark form, satisfaction theology is given full confessional expression in the third verse of "How Great Thou Art":

When I think that God his Son not sparing
Sent him to die, I scarce can take it in.
That on the Cross my burden gladly bearing,
He bled and died to take away my sin.

I like creative and stirring arrangements of "How Great Thou Art." I am very happy to sing strongly about how we can wander through the woods and glades and praise "all the worlds Thy Hands have made." And in the final verse, I sing more loudly than anyone about "when Christ shall come, with shout of acclamation and take me home what joy shall fill my soul." It is just verse 3. Because I take popular theology seriously, I cannot and will not sing it, because I hope it, and the bloodthirsty God behind it, just isn't true, because what makes God great is that he wants nothing to do with death and its courtiers. God wants life and liberty and joy for us.

Why does this matter? Well, if we keep singing hymns like this, some people may think it is true, may remember it, and want it sung at all their family's baptisms, weddings, funerals, and other rites of passage. And they do. But this hymn gives a very limited version of the truth it is trying to articulate, and the implications it holds regarding where God is to be found in our suffering and pain cannot be underestimated. God's will for Jesus affects everything about how we think God deals with us. If our God wants and sends suffering, even setting up a grisly death for his only beloved Son, then why should we complain when we get a disease, an illness, lose a child or a loved one? We are getting off lightly in comparison to what some claim God wanted from Jesus.

However, Jesus did not simply and only come to die. Rather, Jesus came to live and, as a result of the courageous and radical way he lived his life, and the saving love he embodied for all humanity, he threatened the political, social, and religious authorities of his day so much that they executed him. This is an easier way for us to make sense of the predictions of the passion. Jesus was no clairvoyant; he was a full and true human being and therefore had informed but limited knowledge. His full and true divinity cannot obliterate his humanity or he would be playacting at being human. His divinity is seen in and through the uncompromisingly loving, just, and sacrificial way he lived within the bounds of his humanity.

And think about what we have done to the cross of Christ. Many of us now wear small crosses and crucifixes in rolled gold, platinum, or sterling silver. They dangle around our necks or from our earlobes. I wonder if the Romans had had access to the electric chair rather than the cross, whether we would now have small silver, gold, or platinum electric chairs around our necks or hanging from our earlobes. Furthermore, rather than starting our prayers by signing ourselves with the sign of the cross, we might assume the grip of one in an electric chair and begin our prayers with "Szszszsz." This provocative and contemporary image brings home to us what Paul calls the "scandal of the cross" (1 Cor 1:18–26). The cross of Christ is not a fashion accessory, no matter how many of them Madonna and Eminem wear. Looking upon it should still take our breath away. Not only because it shows us how far Jesus was prepared to go in establishing his reign of justice and love in this world, but also because it spells out the cost for all of us who follow his Way, speak his Truth, and live his Life. This should be as radical and threatening now as it was in the first century. For those of us who put on a cross, and for everyone who carries one, we want to answer Christ's question, "How far will you go out of love in following me?" with the same answer he gave the Father, and us: "I will go to the end. I will see it through, no matter the cost."

Over the years, when good people ask how a loving God could do such terrible things to them, some Christians will avoid the answer to that question and simply tell them to "offer it up." By this they seem to be saying, "Well, God required Jesus to suffer a torturous death, so you must see in your own suffering and pain God offering you the same cup of suffering as he offered Jesus." It is not that long ago that these ideas had such currency that we "offered up" our suffering for the salvation of souls in purgatory, or for others whose lives we thought offended God. My worry is not that Jesus suffered and died and that so do we, but what sort of image of God emerges from understanding our salvation in terms of the commercial transaction of paying a ransom, or an angry God deriving satisfaction from us "offering up" our suffering and illness and pain, which he has sent to us in the first place.

Another traditional way of understanding our suffering is to say that we are freely uniting our sufferings with the sufferings of Jesus, so they then take on some meaning. If my thoughts on why

Jesus suffered hold true, we could reclaim that style of approach but with an important difference. Rather than the implied belief that it is about the further appeasement of a needy God, which is difficult given that Jesus' sacrifice was once and for all, I find meaning in my suffering by being faithful to Jesus' Way, Truth, and Life when every other instinct in me wants to cut and run. Here I find God in my Gethsemane, enabling me to confront death and destruction and sin head-on, now certain, through the experience of Jesus, that the life of God will have the last word.

Many of the most morally courageous people in history knew that their personal life and liberty were threatened because of what they were saying or how they were living. They may not have known beforehand they would be executed or murdered or assassinated, but they could read the signs of their times well enough to predict that there were serious consequences to the freedom they were embodying and to which they were attracting other people. Sometimes they spoke or wrote about the cost of the stands they took. In this regard, they reflect Jesus Christ. Our martyrs are not Christian versions of suicide bombers. They do not go looking for death in any active sense. That would be the ultimate betrayal of God's gift of life. However, they know that they may die as a result of witnessing to their faith and the demand for justice that must flow from it. In their lives and deaths they follow the pattern of Jesus. He did not seek death for its own sake, but he would not and could not live any other way than faithfully, hopefully, and lovingly. In his day, as in our own, this is immensely threatening to those whose power base is built on values opposed to these virtues. The world continues to silence and sideline people who live out the Christian virtues and values, just as Jesus was thought to be ultimately sidelined in his crucifixion. But God had the last word on the death of Jesus: Life.

Once we replace the question "Why did Jesus die?" with "Why was Jesus killed?" then the last days of Jesus' suffering and death can be seen in an entirely new perspective.

With this new perspective, we can stand before the cross and listen to Jesus in John's Gospel say, "I have come that you may have life, and have it to the full." This life is not about the perfect Son of the perfect Father making the perfect sacrifice to get us back in God's good books, and thereby saving us. Our God does not deal in death, but with life. Everything in the New Testament demonstrates this, even the grand apocalyptic narratives about the end of time, which show the hallmarks of an inspired rabbinic teacher drawing big strokes on the largest of canvases. Jesus did not intend us to take this imagery literally. I assume the experience of judgment will not actually be a livestock muster of sheep and goats. The lesson behind the imagery, however, is a real one for us to learn. God's compassion and love will ultimately see that justice is done. He will hear the cry of the poor and we will be called to account in the next life for what we have done and what we have failed to do in this life.

On Good Friday, we find God-in-Jesus-Christ confronting evil, death, and destruction head-on, and staring it down, so that God's light and life would have the last word in Jesus' life, and through him for all of creation.

9.

A LOVING GOD, HEAVEN, HELL, AND PURGATORY

Given what I have said about Jesus not coming among us primarily and only to die for our sins, but moreover dying at the hands of our sinfulness, then his life, death, and resurrection show us how to live—even through our suffering and death to life eternal. There is no question that God's judgment and condemnation have been presented by some Christians over the millennia as a form of social control, but those days are now gone. If there are some Catholics preaching hellfire and damnation as the reason for faith these days, they must be disappointed that very few people are listening to them or worried about it. The rates of religious practice, which was often the way a believer tried to keep an angry God on his or her side and thereby avoid hell, have plummeted in almost every Western country. However, one of the major shifts in theology over the last fifty years has been from being driven by fear to being drawn by love. I am not a Christian, a Catholic, a Jesuit, or a priest because I am trying to "save my soul" from hell. I do what I do because it is my response to a loving God's invitation to faith, hope, and love.

Even when heaven, hell, and purgatory were presented graphically, there were always problems with the literalness of the images.

Classical theology has always held that in eternal life there will not be time and space, mind and body. Heaven is about transcending the bounds of earth. So even when preachers talked about "fire and brimstone" and "physical pangs," it was a poetic way to describe the indescribable because we cannot undergo physical torments if we don't have a physical body.

Our Catholic theology about heaven, hell, and purgatory enshrines a profound religious truth—that our life here on earth impacts on our eternal life.

I have confident faith that God would not deny heaven to the many people we know who faithfully, lovingly, and hopefully lived their lives as best as they could. The Scriptures give us confidence in knowing that God does not concern himself with small matters. But what about the individuals and societies whose behavior destroys other people? What about those who never repent of the sexual abuse of a child, their physical and emotional violence, being serial adulterers and murderers? What about those who refuse to share from their excess with those who have nothing in our world? And what about those who don't care or don't want to know about the fallout from their apathy or the consequences involved in the luxury of ignorance? None of these people, none of us, is ever too far from the compassion and forgiveness of God, but I am also convinced that God takes our free decisions on serious matters very seriously.

Before offering some reflections on heaven, hell, and purgatory, let us consider the "soul." If eternal life transcends time and space, mind and body, then we cannot "do time" in purgatory in the traditional sense, and we need to clarify what survives us when we die. Christians have always claimed that while our body dies, our spirit or soul is what survives and endures.

In an increasingly secular society, it is striking how the word *soul* persists in ordinary conversation. Many nonreligious people use this most religious of terms to describe another person. We often hear how others are lonely, distressed, or lost souls. It can be said that someone has a "beautiful soul" or that a piece of music, a painting, or other works of art "stirred my soul." We describe mellow jazz as "soulful" and still alert others with an SOS, "save our souls." These uses of the word reinforce St. Thomas Aquinas's teaching that the soul makes us human, and sets us apart from other animals. Nearly all the great religions of the world believe in a soul or its equivalent—something that survives the annihilation of the body in death.

It is my view that whatever else might characterize the soul, memory is an integral part of it. Why?

I have done several funerals of people who have suffered from Alzheimer's disease. These are rarely very sad occasions because the family invariably says that they "lost" their loved one months or years ago. This is because their loved one increasingly couldn't remember anyone or anything. We hold to caring for the body from the womb to the tomb, because we believe that human dignity must always be respected. There are now theories about how even the memories of the circumstances of our conception and birth have a bearing on the way we live our lives. It is also apparent that, even when people seem to have lost their memory or are unconscious, there is some recognition of some things at a very deep level.

Soul as memory means that when I meet God face-to-face, I will remember who I am and how I lived, and God will remember me. It's also a comfort for us to think that we will be reunited with those we have loved and who have died before us, because we remember each other.

This is not the last word on the matter, since it raises the question of the humanity of those whom we do not think can remember anything. Are they any less human? I would say that every human being has inalienable rights because they may have memory at their deepest level, and because we know in faith that each and every one is known and remembered by God from conception to death.

So what happens after our soul leaves our body, "commended to the mercy of God," as we used to say? Well, the great parable of God's mercy is the best place to start.

In the story of the prodigal son, we have the worst kid in town making a return and being received by his foolishly loving father.

Rather than think of heaven, hell, and purgatory as places where we do time, imagine if they are experiences or states. I wonder if a goodly number of souls, people who have done their best on earth, according to their lights, make the journey home. The

Father rushes out to greet them. They start their speech, but the loving Father cuts them off, and welcomes them home. That has to be the experience of heaven—welcomed to the eternal banquet!

However, some make the journey home and start the speech, which the loving Father allows them to finish—such has been the enormity of their deliberately chosen, free, and seriously destructive behavior toward others and themselves in this world. At the end of the speech they are forgiven, now fully aware of the gravity of their sinfulness, and its impact. And it costs us to say "I'm sorry" and it costs the Father to forgive (like a husband or wife who genuinely forgives the other for adultery). That might be purgatory—an experience in cleansing, of being purged, not in anger or suffering, but in love—painful love as it might be.

And for a very few who have deliberately and knowingly rejected God throughout their whole lives—God in all his forms: in faith, hope, and love—they make the journey to the Father and come face-to-face with pure love. They do not start the speech, they are not welcomed in, because God respects their freedom so much that he allows them to do what they have done all their lives—see love and walk away. That has to be hell—to know love, to have glimpsed it, and still turn around and walk away because they always have. The ultimate absence: a remembering soul that saw love and chose otherwise.

10.

WOMEN'S LEADERSHIP

In speaking with young Catholic women, it is rare that this issue does not emerge strongly for many of them as a problem in their life of faith. In nearly every other sphere of life, women are, at least theoretically, and now as enshrined by law in many countries, able to hold any office of principal authority in any institution other than religious ones. Certainly, some women and men have walked away from a faith in a so-called male God, and some from the Catholic Church, in particular, because they see it as inherently discriminatory.

Though the status of women is vastly different throughout the world, and sometimes very tragic in some cultures, even within these differing social expectations, St. Pope John Paul II said that women's rights to dignity and human flourishing are given by God and should always be defended by the Church.[11] Given the differing social expectations, and even though the issues are larger than ordination, current debates, both inside and outside the Church, often center on the Church stating that it cannot—has no authority to—ordain women to the priesthood.

The following is a brief summary, which hardly conveys all the arguments presented in the libraries of books written on both sides of this debate. There are six main reasons the Church says it has no power to ordain women: first, Jesus did not ordain any women—the first apostles were all male; second, the all-male priesthood has been an unbroken tradition in the Church's history; third, in sacramental liturgies, the priest acts in the name and person of Jesus—having a male priest establishes a clearer iconography or identification between the priest and Jesus; fourth, while women and men are created equal by God, they have differing gender-specific roles, and to confuse these is to harm the balance of our human condition; fifth, the priesthood should not be seen as an office of power to be obtained and used, but as an order of self-sacrificing service; finally, the Church has been a place where women are not oppressed but where their many and manifest gifts have flourished and been celebrated from Mary, the Mother of God, who is first among (all) the saints, to St. Mary Magdalene, who was the "Apostle to the Apostles," to an array of mystics, saints, founders, martyrs, and scholars.

The critics of these arguments claim the following: first, Jesus may have had twelve male apostles, but he had and commissioned many female disciples, some of whom were his most faithful followers. They also challenge that he "ordained" anyone in the way the Church now uses that term and understands that office. Set against the customs of his day, his attitudes and practices toward women and their leadership were radical. Second, the argument of an unbroken tradition of an all-male liturgical leadership is not as watertight as some claim. There is some evidence of women presiding over house churches, Mary Magdalene and Junia are called apostles, and women were deacons for several centuries. Third, at sacramental liturgies, the priest acts in the name and person of the risen Christ, in whom "there is no longer Jew or Greek, there is no longer slave or free, there is no longer male and female; for all of you are one in Christ Jesus" (Gal 3:28). While the Church has let go of Jesus' culture and religion as prerequisites for Christian ordination, gender, apparently, remains the only nonnegotiable. Fourth, given that we no longer read Genesis literally, the gender roles that emerge there should not be absolutized, but should rather be interpreted as a theological construction around social determinations. Fifth, there is nothing wrong in talking about access to governance when it combines the right and just use of power as well as modeling self-sacrificing service. Finally, for all the Church's rhetoric about the great gifts of women, and especially about motherhood, there has not been a corresponding and meaningful harnessing of their gifts for leadership at every level of the Church's life.

While the judgment of a male cleric might be seen to be overly defensive of the Church's position, there is an important distinction to be made in this debate between ordination and leadership. Many of the greatest women in the Church's history have had to put up with appalling discrimination from male Church officials of their day. The only historical comfort we can draw from what they suffered is that their detractors are now forgotten to history, but each of them has, or is in the process of being, declared a saint, and rightly so.

It is important to keep the distinction between ordination and leadership in perspective. While ordination gives a priest sacramental and structural power, it does not necessarily bestow upon him the gift of leadership that is endorsed by a leader's followers. There are some priests who may be ordained, but they lead no one anywhere. There are women who have never and will never be ordained, but their leadership is inspiring. If we look beyond sacramental leadership—and I concede that is a central reality of the Catholic Church's life—and examine education, healthcare, welfare, pastoral care, and spirituality, we find that in almost every Western country in the world, women's leadership is indispensable. In fact, if women stopped leading and working in all these ministries, the entire mission and daily ministry of the Church would come to a halt. It might be a good thing if the women of the Church went on strike one week in order to remind the men who it is that are actually running this "show" in and through their sometimes heroic, self-sacrificing service.

Similarly, it is important that we recognize the equal dignity of women and men created in the image and likeness of God and their complementarity and mutuality, so that it translates into the active participation of women throughout all levels of decision making in the Church, a reexamination of the nature of non-priestly ministry with the exploration of more inclusive roles for men and women, and a reform of practices that do not promote the equality of men and women.

Pope Francis seems keen to initiate such a discussion on the role of women in the life of the Church.

Women must have a greater presence in the decision-making areas of the church....[They] cannot be limited to the fact of being an altar server or the president of Caritas, the catechist....No!...We need to create still broader opportunities for a more inclusive female presence in the Church....Demands that the legitimate rights of women be respected, based on the firm conviction that men and women are equal in dignity, present the Church with profound and challenging questions which cannot be lightly evaded.[12]

In fact, in *Amoris Laetitia* ("The Joy of Love") of March 2016, Francis has gone further than any of his other predecessors when the pope said, "I certainly value feminism, but one that does not demand uniformity or negate motherhood. For the grandeur of women includes all the rights derived from their inalienable human dignity but also from their feminine genius, which is essential to society" (no. 173) and

I would like to stress the fact that, even though significant advances have been made in the recognition of women's rights and their participation in public life, in some countries much remains to be done to promote these rights....There are those who believe that many of today's problems have arisen because of feminine emancipation. This argument, however, is not valid, "it is false, untrue, a form of male chauvinism." The equal dignity of men and women makes us rejoice to see old forms of discrimination disappear, and within families there is a growing reciprocity. If certain forms of feminism have arisen which we must consider inadequate, we must nonetheless see in the women's movement the working of the Spirit for a clearer recognition of the dignity and rights of women. (no. 54)

Maybe we will soon head in the direction outlined by Cardinal Martini[13] and Bishop Wcela in calling for women to be ordained deacons; that is yet to be seen.

Ordaining women as deacons who have the necessary personal, spiritual, intellectual and pastoral qualities would give their indispensable role in the life of the church a new degree of official recognition, both in their ministry and in their direct connection to their diocesan bishop for assignments and faculties. In addition to providing such women with the grace of the sacrament, ordination would enable them to exercise diaconal service in the teaching, sanctifying, and governing functions of the church; it would also make it possible for them to hold ecclesiastical offices now limited to those in sacred orders."[14]

Future discussion about women becoming cardinals is both theologically and theoretically possible.[15] Regardless of this discussion, it is incontestable that women should participate more and more at every level of decision making: locally, nationally, and internationally. Rather than walk away from the Church, young women will hopefully stay, and name and shame any discrimination they experience in God's name, enabling all of us to create a more inclusive and empowering church for them and their daughters and sons.

ST. MARY MACKILLOP (1842–1909)

Maybe one of the best examples of how women have paid a price for their leadership in Christianity is Mary Mackillop. Strictly speaking, Mary is known as St. Mary of the Cross. She is Australia's first and at present only canonized Catholic saint. It is striking that most Australians do not use her formal title, but refer to her by her baptismal name. Maybe it has something to do with Australia's more relaxed and informal style, for even after she was canonized, many Australians drop the "Saint" altogether when we speak of her—because good friends rarely stand on ceremony.

It's not that Mary did not know about being crucified; she certainly did. She gives comfort to every sane, rebellious prophet in the Church and the world.

While she may have set out to become a saint, something

all baptized people are told by St. Paul to desire, she was a most reluctant prophet. A teacher by profession, she was appalled by the poverty in rural Australia and knew that education was one of the great keys to true freedom, especially for the deprived people of the Australian outback. In 1866, with her priest friend and adviser, Fr. Julian Tenison Woods, she founded the Sisters of St. Joseph of the Sacred Heart for the education of poor children. Within five years, 130 sisters were running more than forty schools and welfare institutions across South Australia and Queensland. Within a hundred years (along with the Sisters of Mercy), the "Joeys" (as they are affectionately called) were in every tin-pot place in the country.

In 1866, Australia was not yet a federation; that occurred in 1901. However, decades before that event, Mary Mackillop wanted her sisters to be free from the interference of local bishops and to respond to national needs. So she opted for a central, national government for her Congregation. Most of the Australian bishops did not like it, especially Bishop Sheil of Adelaide, who, believing false allegations that Mary was financially incompetent and an alcoholic, formally excommunicated her on September 22, 1871.

Sheil was certainly not alone. Of the fourteen bishops in Australia and New Zealand in 1871, eleven wrote to Rome against Mary and her sisters. Only three bishops supported her, and they all belonged to a religious order themselves. Today, none of these men are known, except to historians, but the woman they condemned is given to us as a model of universal holiness. In a dominantly patriarchal church, St. Mary Mackillop was loyal in her dissent, strong in hope, magnificent in faith, and unfailing in her forgiveness of her enemies.

With the excommunication lifted on February 23, 1872, Mary had to set about protecting her work and her sisters. This was aided and abetted through an unlikely conspiracy between a Jew, a Presbyterian, and two Jesuits. (That's starting to sound like the beginning of a joke!)

One of Mary's great patrons and friends was Mrs. Joanna Barr-Smith, a devout Presbyterian, who helped finance Mary's first mother house in Adelaide and paid for her tombstone. To have a Protestant benefactor may have been bad enough at the time, but to call her "my very dear friend," as Mary often did, was dangerous in sectarian nineteenth-century Australia.

One of Mary's other good friends was Emmanuel Solomon, a Jewish man, who was transported to Australia as a convict for theft in 1818, and later became a successful businessman, parliamentarian, and philanthropist. He admired Mary's work. When she was excommunicated, it was Mrs. Barr-Smith and Mr. Solomon who paid for her first-class ticket on the boat from Adelaide to Rome to petition Pope Pius IX to approve and protect her community of sisters.

Mary's younger brother, Donald, was educated by the Jesuits and later joined the Order, and her own spiritual director in Adelaide was an Austrian Jesuit, Josef Tappeiner. When the twenty-nine-year-old Mary was excommunicated, Fr. Tappeiner was so appalled at what he thought was an invalid and immoral act, that he and another Austrian Jesuit, Fr. Joannes Hinteroecker, gave Mary the sacraments in spite of the bishop saying that anyone who communicated with her would suffer the same penalty.

Mary arrived in Rome in 1873. Father Tappiener had paved the way for her with introductions to his old Jesuit friend, Fr. Anton Anderledy, who was an assistant to, and later became, the Superior General of the Jesuits. It was Fr. Anderledy who assisted Mary through the Vatican's processes for approving her constitutions to gain papal protection for her sisters from local bishops, and finally, to be personally received by Pope Pius IX.

I only know of one other person who has gone from excommunication to canonization, another woman: St. Joan of Arc. In her case, it tragically took 489 years. Mary Mackillop took 139 years.

One of the least-known chapters in her life, however, is also the one that has the greatest contemporary resonance. In 1870, Mary's religious sisters accused their local assistant parish priest of sexual offenses "committed frequently and with many" against children and women in the confessional. There was an investigation and the priest was found guilty of the offenses. He was sent back to Europe. The parish priest was also condemned for "turning a blind eye" to the abuse.[16] He was removed from the parish and sent to the Bishop's House in Adelaide. Saint Mary Mackillop supported the denunciation of these priests, but it incurred the wrath of the sacked parish priest, who, the following year, would then be one of Bishop Sheil's closest advisers regarding her excommunication.

In St. Mary Mackillop we have an outstanding Christian, who refused to be mastered by her religious masters; a person open to ecumenism and interreligious dialogue, who knew that the best way to tear down sectarianism and religious bigotry is simply through friendship; a teacher, who believed that education is one of the best paths to human and spiritual liberation; a passionate advocate, who had to learn how to use her networks to win both the battle and the war; and an adult who paid a terrible price because she would not be silent in the face of sexual abuse by clergy.

11.

THE CHALLENGE OF THE GOSPEL

Every major study of belief and unbelief says that for many people it is not only a deity that is the major stumbling block to religious faith, but also the lives of religious individuals and collectives who claim to follow that God. It is chastening to think that the Church, universally and locally, can be the greatest obstacle to anyone believing in the God we proclaim. It is a good challenge to practice what we preach and to follow Jesus' service, humility, and simplicity. It seems that Pope Francis's example has gone some way in this regard.

It is true that Jesus was a poor man who preached a gospel about lifting up the poor, the marginalized, and the oppressed, and who said that not only do we have an obligation to share, but that we will be happiest when we are free of the possessions that keep us from loving God and our neighbor. He also knew that love of money was one of the greatest dangers to us losing our very selves. There is no question that for the first three hundred years of the Christian Church's life, it lived the simplicity Jesus lived. In fact, given that many people died for their Christian faith, their witness to a sacrificial life is above reproach.

The defining change, for good and for ill, comes after Constantine's vision in AD 312 that led him to convert to Christianity and use his new faith as a unifying force in his empire. By 380, Christianity had become the state religion. On the positive side, this meant that Christians were no longer martyred for their faith. On the downside, the Christian Church now received imperial patronage, had confiscated property returned to it, and gained—and sometimes abused—civil prestige and power. We can easily see why, after generations of martyrs and persecutions, Christians saw this development as a sign of God's blessing. With the demise of the Western Roman Empire in 476, when Romulus Augustus was deposed, the Church began to fill the temporal and spiritual vacuum in the West, and became a threat to the power of the emperor of the Eastern Empire.

In fairness, the Christian Church is the only single institution in Western society to have survived so long. Today, therefore, it is easy to judge what later became the Roman Catholic Church and its subsequent claim on or over power and wealth as a betrayal of what Jesus proclaimed. It certainly was a betrayal, but it also provided social stability and cohesion in very desolate times. For over a thousand years, there was a varied but often mutually dysfunctional relationship between temporal powers and the popes of the Roman Church, which takes on all the trappings of the earthly kingdom Jesus rejected. Innocent III (1198–1216) and Boniface VIII (1294–1303) embody the culmination of papal power over church, state, appointments, land, armies, and wealth.

So much for history, except that without noting this development, it is impossible to understand where we are now. We have no idea how wealthy the Catholic Church actually is. Against the monolithic institution that many assume the Church to be, it is, in fact, a communion of churches, albeit one where the pope "has full, supreme and universal power" (Vatican Council II, *Lumen Gentium*, no. 22). Nevertheless, what makes me Catholic is not any personal affection for a particular pope, but the more ancient tradition of being in communion (literally, we can receive the same holy communion) with my local bishop, who is, in turn, in communion with the Bishop of Rome. At the time of writing, there were 2,946 dioceses in the Catholic world, and though they have to annually report to Rome on their local church, many would not know the actual wealth of all the local holdings. Suffice it to say, some dioceses are very wealthy and some are desperately poor. Being private, not-for-profit institutions, almost none of these dioceses have to give full financial disclosure to civil authorities. No doubt, this will change in the years to come.

In 2012, *The Economist* estimated that the Catholic Church in the United States was worth around $170 billion, of which $150 billion was estimated to be in the assets and real estate of Catholic healthcare, welfare, and educational institutions. Trying to put a value on the Vatican City State is nearly impossible. The best estimate is around $10 to $15 billion. It has 15 percent of the value of the listed shares on the Italian stock market, which is thought to be valued at $1.2 billion. The annual running budget of the Vatican is approximately $325 million, with $115 million of that coming from the five million tourists who enter one or more of the museums each year. The shortfall is made up from investments and donations from dioceses around the world. It employs 2,800 employees. It is a vast enterprise and a long way from the simplicity and poverty of the first community around Jesus.

No matter how much we try to ignore it, or play it down, the call to simplicity of lifestyle, detachment, and sharing what we have are essential elements in the teaching of Jesus, the way he lived his own life, and they still challenge us today.

On the other side of the ledger, it is good to remember that the wealth of the Church is not only and simply about power for its own sake. For a start, the Vatican would need to financially assist hundreds of its dioceses to provide local services, on every level, for believer and unbeliever alike. In many countries, the Church, albeit sometimes with the support of tax-free concessions also granted to other charities, is, outside government, the single largest provider of healthcare, welfare, and education in that nation. Many millions of people a year, regardless of their religious, social, or economic backgrounds, are served by the money raised by Caritas, which is itself a confederation of 164 Roman Catholic relief agencies in two hundred countries; as well as Catholic Mission; Catholic Relief Services in the United States; the Catholic Agency for Overseas Development in the United Kingdom; the Pontifical Mission Societies, operating in 120 countries; the Missionary Childhood Association; Jesuit Refugee Service; Mercy Refugee Service; and the St. Vincent de Paul Society, just to name a few of the hundreds and hundreds of relief and service organizations sponsored or promoted by the Catholic Church.

Even though there is a valid argument that the Vatican museums could sell the art and give the money to the poor (though it would be hard to get Michelangelo off the roof and walls of the Sistine Chapel), I am not sure it is the only valid argument. Last year the Vatican Museum was the fifth most visited gallery in the world, and those of us who have been there know most people visit simply to see the Sistine Chapel. However, even if the holdings were sold, they would almost certainly go into the hands of private buyers, thirty-nine of the top fifty of whom last year were from China. Most of the top fifty buyers do not donate or show their works in public galleries. As complex as the commissioning and acquisition of our Catholic artistic heritage may be, at least now it can be enjoyed by generation after generation of ordinary people. The sale of it now would be good for temporary public relations for the Vatican, but it would have minimal impact on the life of the poor.

So while extraordinary events in history, along with criminal abuse of power and mutual alliances, have left us with the legacy of the real estate and art and architecture we own, selling it all in our following of Jesus in poverty is one option. Using all the resources at our disposal, not only to feed the poor, but to change the international structures that keep them that way, is another option. The real stumbling block is learning from the avarice and triumphalism of some of the previous generations of the Church. Living simply with what we need rather than what we want, sharing everything with the poor, who are at the center of the gospel, and being a voice for the voiceless in many circles in which the Church lives might be the even bigger and more exciting challenges.

In living memory for some of us, one of the best examples of following Christ poor is Mother Teresa.

ST. TERESA OF CALCUTTA (1910–1997)

Christopher Hitchens did a hatchet job on Mother Teresa. The long character assassination that is *The Missionary Position* could be fairly summarized as portraying Mother Teresa as a fanatic, a fundamentalist, a fraud, and a friend of poverty because she was against abortion, contraception, and divorce, and that she was theologically dogmatic, had blind faith, and enjoyed "the cult of a mediocre human personality."[17] In this context, I do not think it is mean to note that some of the things Christopher Hitchens observes in Mother Teresa can be found, albeit in different ways, in him and his own aggressive atheism: fanaticism, fundamentalism, dogmatism, blind faith in his own version of reality, and enjoying the cult of personality from his own disciples. This seeming psychological projection, rejection of religious belief, legitimate disagreement over the ways to alleviate poverty, and fundamental clash of political ideology is exacerbated by the fact that Hitchens could not abide that Mother Teresa's fame enabled her to raise money to fund her causes and works.

Having largely worked in poor obscurity for twenty years, there is scant evidence that she was working for the poor for the sake of her own ego and for financial reward. It is true, however, that once fame came her way, she used it to speak about social and political issues of concern to her and the Catholic Church, and to raise funds for her work and the quickly expanding Missionaries of Charity. I don't know another activist who would not do the same for their causes and organizations. Her style could be abrasive, her administration was haphazard, her accounting was far from systematic, and her educational and clinical care was, and is, basic, but no one has been able to prove that she or her sisters siphoned off any money to a Swiss bank account whereby she or others lived in luxury, or that, because her care was rudimentary, it was not better than the alternative for the poorest of the poor. Others may not like her unremitting stance on what is now called reproductive rights, but she was a Catholic of her time and in lockstep with a stark presentation of the Church's teaching.

On reading Hitchens's book, I was left asking what systematic improvements had Hitchens ever achieved in his lifetime on behalf of, for, or with the poor, anywhere. I am unaware of a single achievement. Hitchens's criticism is so extreme he does not make a single positive comment about her. Conversely, I have seen the good work Mother Teresa's sisters have done, and still do, for the poor in several parts of the world. Today, there are 4,500 sisters in 131 countries. Admittedly, my major personal criticism of her concerns how she tended to romanticize the degradation of grinding poverty. In October 1981, on a visit to Washington, DC, she said, "I think it is very beautiful for the poor to accept their lot, to share it with the passion of Christ. I think the world is being much helped by the suffering of the poor people."[18] I can see how this fits into a traditional Catholic theology of reparation and sin, which has developed considerably in recent decades, for while people who are poor have inalienable rights and dignity, poverty is an evil to be eradicated. At the risk of criticizing Blessed Teresa for what she did not do, I am reminded of Helder Camara's famous comment: "When I give food to the poor, they call me a saint. When I ask why the poor have no food, they call me a communist." It is a rare human being who is good at both.

However, there are several unusual things about Mother Teresa's life that are inspiring. The first is that she was a woman who knew what it was to be pushed from pillar to post. Anjezë Gonxhe Bojaxhiu was born into the Ottoman Empire, but in her lifetime she became, in turn, Serbian, Bulgarian, Yugoslav, and Indian, and if she were able to return to her birthplace now, she would discover that she was now a Macedonian. "By blood, I am Albanian. By citizenship, an Indian. By faith, I am a Catholic nun. As to my calling, I belong to the world. As to my heart, I belong entirely to the Heart of Jesus."

Inspired to become a missionary sister, it is not clear how or why she chose the Institute of the Blessed Virgin Mary (IBVM), commonly called the Loreto Sisters. They did not work in her country of birth, but she did know that they worked in India. First, however, she went to the IBVM in Ireland to learn English for her work in India. In 1929, she was sent to the novitiate of the Sisters of Loreto at Darjeeling.

Maybe the constant change of her citizenship, and the extraordinary amount of travel she did for a woman of her time, explains in some measure her later attachment to rigid structures while being on the move.

In 1931, she took her vows and was appointed to St. Mary's College at Calcutta for the next fifteen years. Although she was happy teaching relatively well-off girls, it was the poor, literally beyond her gate, who called her. By 1946, she was sure she was meant to serve them in some way.

By 1948, she was given permission to live outside the convent. She dressed in a blue-bordered sari and founded a school for the often-homeless children in the poorest parts of Calcutta, teaching them basic literacy. She was soon joined by other women who wanted to work with her, most of whom were her former students. On October 7, 1950, the Missionaries of Charity were officially established. On April 12, 1952, twelve sisters took first vows as Missionaries of Charity and Mother Teresa took final vows. That same year Mother Teresa opened Kalighat, her first home for the dying in Calcutta. She came to national prominence in India in 1948 when Prime Minister Nehru praised her work with the poor. She came to international attention primarily after Malcolm Muggeridge's BBC documentary about her work in 1968, and his 1972 book, *Something Beautiful for God*.

In 2007, *Mother Teresa: Come Be My Light* was published. It consists of the letters and other correspondences between Mother Teresa, her confessors, and superiors over sixty-six years. The editor, Rev. Brian Kolodiejchuk, says that it is "proof of the faith-filled perseverance that he sees as her most spiritually heroic act." I have mixed feelings about this publication, mainly because Mother Teresa explicitly asked her spiritual director to "please destroy any letters or anything I have written." She never wanted anyone to read these letters. However, they do reveal an extraordinary insight into her life that makes her even more inspiring.

In 1953, she wrote, "There is such terrible darkness within me, as if everything was dead. It has been like this more or less from the time I started the work....In my heart there is no faith—no love—no trust—there is so much pain—the pain of longing, the pain of not being wanted. I want God with all the powers of my soul—and yet there between us—there is terrible separation. I don't pray any longer." Later, she says, "In my soul I feel just that terrible pain of loss, of God not wanting me—of God not being God—of God not existing."[19]

There is no evidence in her letters that this sense of God's absence ever lifted. In fact, she kept questioning and doubting her faith and that she was doing the right thing for the rest of her life. Her ministry held no consolation for her. Except for her spiritual advisers, no one knew this. Everyone assumed the opposite to be true. In this context, what is extraordinary is that she just kept going, doing her work for the poor in the hope that it was pleasing to God.

My friend and colleague, James Martin, SJ, has insightfully observed,

> Few of us, even the most devout believers, are willing to leave everything behind to serve the poor. Consequently, Mother Teresa's work can seem far removed from our daily lives. Yet, in its relentless and even obsessive questioning, her life intersects with that of the modern atheist and agnostic. "If I ever become a saint," she wrote, "I will surely be one of 'darkness.'"…Mother Teresa's ministry with the poor won her the Nobel Prize and the admiration of a believing world. Her ministry to a doubting modern world may have just begun.[20]

Mother Teresa died the same week as Diana, Princess of Wales. They were two of the most identifiable women of their day. After her car accident, understandably, the world never saw a new photograph of Diana again. One of the most glamorous women in the world was hidden from public sight. Mother Teresa had many gifts, but no one would ever have described her as glamorous. In death, and after she was embalmed, Mother Teresa was permanently on display, even during her funeral eight days after she died.

While she was alive, there was one revelation after another about Diana but, mercifully, nothing much more has emerged since her tragic death. A lot of ink was spilled on Mother Teresa while she was alive too, but only in death have we discovered how long and lonely her life of faith actually was. Because of that, she becomes an even more illuminating person.

12.

RELIGION, POLITICS, AND LAW

Nearly every ethical system in the world, religious or secular, outlines fundamental principles of our shared humanity, our interdependence on one another, and respect for the natural order as a way to live peacefully together and to avoid suffering—which is a perfectly good place for dialogue to begin.

While some atheists and secular humanists are obsessed about religion, others could not care less about it until religion has an impact on an issue of public policy with which they disagree. Of the thirty-four OECD countries in the world—Australia, Austria, Belgium, Brazil, Canada, Chile, Czech Republic, Denmark, Estonia, Finland, France, Germany, Greece, Hungary, Iceland, Ireland, Israel, Italy, Japan, Luxembourg, Mexico, Netherlands, New Zealand, Norway, Poland, Portugal, Russia, Slovak Republic, Slovenia, South Korea, Spain, Sweden, Switzerland, Turkey, United Kingdom, and the United States of America—all, except four, have long and complex associations with Christianity. Given that we only have a few atheistic nations with which to compare and contrast, it can be asserted that Christianity has formed them for the better more than the worse. Furthermore, other religions are significant in the other four countries: Judaism is the predominant religion of Israel; 99 percent of Turkey is Muslim; 93 percent of the population in Japan identify themselves as either Shinto or Buddhist; and in South Korea, over 58 percent are either Buddhist or Christian, while 46.5 percent of all Koreans state they have no religion. Interestingly, even in countries where there is a large number who say they hold no religion, and in the midst of ongoing debate, some of these nations have a state church: Greece, Denmark, Iceland, Norway, and the United Kingdom. Other OECD countries have special constitutional arrangements for one Christian denomination: Poland, Spain, Finland, Sweden, and twenty-four of the twenty-six cantons in Switzerland. Germany, Austria, and Italy have no formal recognition of any religion in their constitutions; but the state does collect a controversial church tax to support religious activities, as does Denmark, Sweden, Finland, Iceland, and all the twenty-six cantons in Switzerland.

The argument on the right role of religion in public policy, therefore, is more complex than it first appears. If Abraham Lincoln is right in saying that "democracy is the government of the people, by the people, for the people," then public policy must reflect the majority view. At the time of writing, France, the Czech Republic, Germany, and South Korea are the four OECD countries where atheists are approaching 30 percent or more of their respective populations. The number of citizens who state that they have no belief is growing significantly in all countries. However, for now, the majority of all OECD countries profess to have some form of religious belief. Therefore, in a democracy, religious believers are fully entitled to participate in the process of political debate and have a hand in shaping the laws that flow from it. It is also true that some religious adherents may disagree with their church's position on one or several issues of the common good. The legalization of illicit drugs, pornography, avoidance of taxation, software piracy, euthanasia, environmental issues, abortion, just distribution of wealth, contraception, rights of workers, adultery, IVF, homosexuality, and immigration issues are just some of the debates I have had with practicing Catholics who have differing views from the official teaching of the Catholic Church.

Two extremes are to be avoided: first, a theocracy, where religious law is the only law of the land. There are only three theocracies left in the world: the Holy See, Iran, and Tibet. Sharia law, however, is followed in Afghanistan, Iran, Mauritania, Saudi Arabia, Somalia, Sudan, Yemen, and some Islamic states within Nigeria. Second, it is equally disturbing for a pluralistic democracy to stifle debate among its citizens. This is not to say that religions should be accorded any special privilege in political debate. Our advocacy for any social policy should rise or fall on the basis of the arguments and its contribution for the common good, regardless of its religious motivations. Religions in Western democracies are now in the game of winning hearts and minds on the basis of their ability to intelligently and truthfully persuade, counsel, and warn their fellow citizens in regard to a particular choice and its potential consequences. The same status should be afforded to all other parties in the debate as well, and then the decisions left to what we hope would be a well-informed legislature.

However, if the wide resentment of those with no religion grows to such a point that all Christian aspects of most OECD countries were dismantled, then it could have far-reaching and maybe unforeseen implications. St. Valentine's Day, named for a third-century Roman martyr who died out of love for Christ, would have to be renamed Cupid's Day, except Cupid was the Greek god of love. The Feasts of Christmas, Good Friday, and Easter, and the public holidays surrounding them, would need to be dropped or transferred or rebranded as secular public commemorations. All references to the Christmas season—the exchange of Christmas gifts, trees, carols, cribs, and dinners—would have to be publically abandoned. Any childcare center that receives any public funding would need to jettison the Christmas nativity play. Professor Dawkins might be sad to see some of that go: "Nor do I shy away from singing the familiar and much loved Christmas songs that I sang for years in choir or at home. Silent Night still can bring a tear to my eye because it recalls memories of childhood."[21] Even Santa Claus would have to be reinvented, since he is based on the fourth-century St. Nicholas, bishop of Myra, who started the practice of giving gifts to the poor in his parish on Christmas Eve around AD 365.

All references to God on secular coats of arms, money, and in all oaths of allegiance, and vows to tell the truth "so help me God" would have to be dismissed. There could be no swearing on a Bible, ever, and no religious prayers uttered anywhere in the civic arena. National songs and hymns would need a makeover so that God would no longer be saving the queen, defending New Zealand, or making Canada glorious and free. Presumably, this would be the end of the taxpayer-funded British royal coronations, funerals, and weddings in the Church of England, which are very popular public broadcasts around the world, because they would now have to be private religious events.

All references directly related to the cross of Christ would have to be changed: the Red Cross, the Victoria Cross, the Distinguished Service Cross, and the Cross of Valor do not owe their origins to any old cross but to the one upon which Jesus died. Even Hollywood would need to be renamed, because in 1886 it was called that by the devout Methodist, Mrs. H. H. Wilcox, after the cross of Christ.[22] We would need new secular symbols as the Star of David, Christian crosses, and crescents on civic flags and banners were dropped.

No doubt, choirs and orchestras that receive any share of government funding or assistance would not be allowed to perform any type of religious music, including "We Shall Overcome" and "Free at last, free at last, thank God Almighty I'm free at last," given that they are gospel songs. Most of Bach would be banned too. All religious art, including indigenous religious art and artifacts, would have to be withdrawn from public view or sold to private collectors. Furthermore, public libraries could raise money for the poor by selling off all their religious volumes, starting with their antiquarian Bibles.

No one should be publicly called a godparent anymore. The state would no longer recognize religious weddings as civil events, so the religious couple would have to have two ceremonies, as is done in France. There could be no state funerals, memorial services of days, or mourning from "national cathedrals." Military chaplains would need to be privatized because they are often on the public payroll. And all religious schools, healthcare institutions, social services, and Third World development agencies would be barred from receiving any state aid, no matter what good they do, because in a secular world it can't be supported if done in God's name. Consequently, the state would need to bear the burden of seeing a dramatic shrinkage of the biggest nongovernment provider of healthcare, welfare, and education in many countries. Sporting groups called the demons, devils, saints, angels, friars, cardinals, or crusaders may need a name change. Any Christian religious procession, a peal from the belfry, a call to prayer from a minaret, the blast of the shofar, and the ringing of the Buddhist bonshō and especially the enormous ōgane could be outlawed as civil disturbances. Finally, phrases with biblical and religious origins might have to be dropped, like talking of a "Good Samaritan," a "prodigal son," a "doubting Thomas," or referring to a meal seemingly prepared from nowhere as the "loaves and the fish."

Does all this sound absurd? It could be. I hope it is. Earlier, I admonished people who were theologically adolescent, all or nothing, and also stated that extreme cases do not prove principles, so I do not want to do either of those things here, except to say that in France, one of the most secular countries on earth, the burqa has now been legally banned, and in the United Kingdom, Canada, and Italy, there are legal cases against individuals wearing crosses and crucifixes in public. Furthermore, there has been fierce opposition to any religious symbols at the 9/11 memorial, which, especially for the families of the victims, is a monumental cemetery. It is, therefore, not so ridiculous to imagine that some of what we describe above could be outlawed because it offends secular sensibilities.

Unless radical atheists and secular humanists want to cherry-pick the bits of Christianity and other religious influences they like, then the denuded secular world just outlined is bleak. However, I am not alone in thinking that the promised secular order would have its severe limitations. Andrew Murray writes, "My fellow atheist opponents…portrayed the future—if we could only shrug off religion—as a wonderful sunlit upland, where reasonable people would make reasonable decisions in a reasonable world. Is it not at least equally likely that if you keep telling people that they lead meaningless lives in a meaningless universe you might just find yourself with—at best—a vacuous life and a hollow culture? My first exhibit in submission involves turning on a television."[23]

More positively, Charles Taylor sums up the tension within which we now live in regard to the mixed history of religion in society and its undoubted accomplishments in Western culture. "It is reasonable to suppose that cultures that have provided the horizon of meaning for large numbers of human beings, of diverse characters and temperaments, over a long period of time— that have, in other words, articulated their sense of the good, the holy, the admirable—are almost certain to have something that deserves our admiration and respect, even if it is accompanied by much that we have to abhor and reject."[24]

DOROTHY DAY (1897–1980)

If there is a Christian with a mixed history who undoubtedly accomplished so much in the Church through her strong advocacy for broader social justice in the world, then Dorothy is it.

Dorothy Day was born in Brooklyn, New York, on November 8, 1897, into a comfortable family. Although her parents were not religious or churchgoers, Dorothy read the Bible as a child and prayed. She joined the local Episcopal Church choir and was later baptized and confirmed. At college, Dorothy became a journalist and political activist, joining the Socialist Party. She rejected all organized religion. For many years, while fighting causes in the labor movement and for socialist and communist ideas, she had a string of sexual encounters. One resulted in a pregnancy and an abortion. In 1922, she married Barkeley Tober. It lasted a year. In 1925, she moved in with an atheist, Forster Batterham, with whom she had a daughter, Tamar Teresa, born on March 3, 1927. She wanted to have Tamar baptized. Batterham strenuously objected. On December 28, 1927, Tamar was baptized and Dorothy was conditionally baptized into the Catholic Church. It split her common law marriage. However, Dorothy remained a friend of Forster for the rest of his life, caring for him in his final illness.

By 1932, Dorothy was writing about unemployment, old age and sick pensions, and the rights and needs of mothers and children for the Catholic journal *Commonweal*. In 1934, she met Peter Maurin, the man she says founded the Catholic Worker, and she worked on its newspaper. She moved into a Catholic Worker House and continued writing, speaking, advocating, and being arrested for her defense of the poor, Catholic social teaching, and pacifism. She died of a heart attack on November 29, 1980.

Dorothy Day's cause to be declared a saint began formally in 2000. For some people, it has been too slow. Many think that her many sexual partners, failed marriage, and the break with the father of her child before her conversion make for a tough case.

It could also be argued that while Dorothy showed due respect to Catholic bishops, they were not beyond her scarifying wit and commentary when they did or said anything she could not reconcile with the highest ideals of Catholic social teaching.

It is true that Dorothy Day did not often speak publicly about her abortion or on this particular right-to-life issue. She was, however, the lead signatory to the Catholic Peace Fellowship Statement on Abortion on June 28, 1974:

> We reject categorically the Supreme Court's argument that abortion is an exclusively private matter to be decided by the prospective mother and her physician.... Indeed, we insist that these positions are all of one piece, stemming from what Albert Schweitzer called, "reverence for life," and the consequent obligation to oppose any policy or practice which would give one human being the right to determine whether or not another shall be permitted to live. For many years we have urged upon our spiritual leaders the inter-relatedness of the life issues, war, capital punishment, abortion, euthanasia and economic exploitation...and to work for their elimination and the establishment of a social order in which all may find it easier to be "fully human."[25]

In 1977, a fellow Catholic worker, Daniel Marshall, asked Dorothy about her abortion. She paused and gently answered, "I don't like to push young people into their sins....You know, I had an abortion. The doctor was fat, dirty and furtive. He left hastily after it was accomplished, leaving me bleeding. The daughter of the landlords assisted me and never said a word of it."[26] In Robert Ellsberg's *All the Way to Heaven*, he cites a letter Dorothy wrote to a young woman where not only did she speak of her abortion, but also the psychological legacy it left: "Twice I tried to take my own life, and the dear Lord pulled me through that darkness—I was rescued from that darkness. My sickness was physical too, since I had had an abortion with bad after-effects, and in a way my sickness of mind was a penance I had to endure."[27]

It seems tragic that such a manifestly good woman who lived with the poor and advocated for them for her entire adult life has to be defended in regard to her sexual history. We have not been so reticent about other saints with complex personal histories before their conversions. Saint Callixtus was an embezzler and political agitator; St. Thomas Becket was a voracious despot; St. Mary of Egypt was a famous seductress; St. Olga was an assassin; St. Vladimir "owned" a harem; St. Philip Howard was a notorious playboy; and, before she saw the light, the Blessed Angela of Foligno's multiple adulteries were scandalous. For St. Augustine of Hippo once said, "There is no saint without a past, no sinner without a future." He knew about both, for, from his own confessions, he tells us that from the age of sixteen "the frenzy gripped me and I surrendered myself entirely to lust," and later he found himself "floundering in the broiling sea of…fornication." We know he fathered at least one child, a son he named Adeodatus.

Saints give testimony to God at work in their lives, not to personal perfection, and so in Dorothy Day we have a saint who knew about the vacuousness of treating sex as a commodity, the failure of relationships, the tragedy for mother and child in abortion, and the feeling that suicide was the only way to stop pain. Rather than rule Dorothy out of sainthood, I admire her even more.

Not that Dorothy wanted to be a saint. "Don't call me a saint. I don't want to be dismissed so easily." I just hope that those who focus so strongly on this chapter of her life equally offer such an exemplary example as hers in their witness to a Christian faith that acts justly. For in that witness, she is one of the great role models. In 1949, she wrote what has become a personal creed of sorts:

> I firmly believe that our salvation depends on the poor. We believe in, "from each according to his ability, to each according to his need." We believe in the communal aspect of property as stressed by the early Christians…. We believe in the constructive activity of the people…. We believe in loving our brothers regardless of race, color or creed and we believe in showing this love by working for better conditions immediately and the ultimate owning by the workers of their means of production. We believe in an economy based on human needs rather than on the profit motive…if we are truly living with the poor, working side by side with the poor, helping the

poor, we will inevitably be forced to be on their side, physically speaking. But when it comes to activity, we will be pacifists, I hope and pray, non-violent resisters of aggression, from whomever it comes, resisters to repression, coercion, from whatever side it comes, and our activity will be the works of mercy. Our arms will be the love of God and our brother."[28]

Even though it has formally started, I think we should abandon the formal process of canonization for someone like Dorothy Day and return to the more ancient Christian practice of creating saints by public acclamation, which gave us such great redeemed sinners and saints like Callixtus, Becket, Mary of Egypt, Olga, Vladimir, Philip Howard, Angela Foligno, and Augustine. Dorothy's canonization will need to be a very simple ceremony, with the poor at the center of it, not outside St. Peter's Basilica, but in the heart of New York City's Times Square.

So while we do not have to be religious to be moral, some of the most heroic human acts of service in every country in the world are done by people motivated by their religious faith. Let me tell you a story about how faith in God can take us to unfamiliar places, and yet when we get there, we can discover God's presence in a new way.

In December 1993, immediately after being ordained, I was appointed as the assistant priest at St. Canice's, the Catholic Parish of King's Cross—the "red light" district of Sydney. It was, as you could imagine, a very colorful parish.

Soon after my ordination, I went to Queensland to say Masses at the Catholic schools, parishes, and communities to which I had belonged over the years at Warwick, Toowoomba, and Brisbane. I returned to King's Cross on Christmas Eve and was told by my seventy-year-old Irish parish priest that I would be presiding at Midnight Mass. What he did not tell me is that while I was away, Esme, our eighty-year-old sacristan, had gone all over to buy every meter of gold lame in Sydney there was to buy to make me a set of vestments for the occasion.

I saw it for the first time when I arrived into the sacristy. Of course, I had to wear it and when I put it on and looked in the mirror, with Esme beaming beside me, I looked like a bloody Christmas tree—wrap lights around me and plug me in and I would have flashed—though not literally!

Midnight Mass was packed to the rafters and, by the way this Catholic congregation sang, it was fairly clear that most people were full of more than one type of Christmas cheer!

Soon after Mass began, five tall men in white blouson shirts walked all the way down the aisle to the only available seat in the church—the very front pew. It was clear that only one of them knew what to do at Mass. He instructed the others to stand, kneel, sit, roll over, and die. (All the things we do at Mass—and we do, in a sense, die with Christ in the Eucharist.)

After Mass, at drinks outside, I went over to these men and welcomed them to the parish. "Hello, I'm Fr. Richard Leonard. I haven't seen you here before and I'd like to wish you a very Happy Christmas." To which one of the five turned to me and said, "Father, if you don't mind me saying so, you wear your frock divinely." At that moment, I turned into the butchest priest in Australia. "I don't get any kicks out of wearing this stuff, you know. I normally get straight back to the sacristy and take it off." And as soon I said that, I really wished I hadn't.

It transpired that my five new parishioners were from the now-defunct *Les Girls Show*. They were at 2 Roslyn Street for twenty-nine years. Saint Canice's is at 28 Roslyn Street. That night they had done the usual show at 10:30 p.m., but as a Christmas special, they still had a late, late show to do at 3:00 a.m. Mark, the only Catholic among them, had convinced his colleagues to "get some religion and come to Midnight Mass."

They had enjoyed Mass so much that Mark suggested that I get a few of the other Jesuits and come up the hill at 3:00 a.m. "Seeing that we came to your show, Father, you should come to ours." I declined the offer, but Mark explained that, in case I changed my mind, there would be tickets waiting for me at the door.

As they were about to walk up the hill, the one who told me that I wore my frock divinely said to me, "Father if ever you want some help to tizz up any of your little church outfits, just let me know, because I am a wonderful designer, and I know I could do a number on you." At that moment, I had visions of coming out from the sacristy the following week in plumes, feathers, and a tiara.

When I got back to the presbytery, I told three young visiting Jesuit students the entire story. It transpired that none of us had been to *Les Girls*. Guess what happened next?

We were late for their show too, but the tickets were waiting for us at the door, there was a table at the back, which suited me just fine, and we were served complimentary drinks. To my relief, no one had seen us enter, and I decided we would be leaving early as well. Saint Ignatius has lots to say about things done in the dark—but we won't go there for the moment.

The girls put on a great show and everything was going along quite nicely until the end. Mark, now in his Marcia persona, went to the microphone to wish everyone a Happy Christmas. He told the audience that to celebrate Christmas, the girls had been to Midnight Mass in between the late shows, and that as a result of that, "we'd like to welcome our local Catholic clergy." With that announcement, a spotlight came on our table! I stood and waved to all my new parishioners.

Marcia then told the crowd that I had sung at Midnight Mass and invited me to "come up here on stage to lead the crowd in a rousing chorus of 'O Come, All Ye Faithful.'" As I walked to the stage, all I could think of was how was I going to explain this to the cardinal, my Irish Jesuit parish priest, my provincial superior (who now happened to be our rector), or worst of all, my mother when she found out!

Do you have any idea who goes to the late, late show of *Les Girls* on Christmas morning—that is, other than young Jesuits!? There I was, not three weeks ordained, at 4:30 a.m. on the stage of *Les Girls* at King's Cross, leading a very dubious group of our compatriots in singing, "O come let us adore him, Christ the Lord."

Within six months of that night, I had buried three of the five men who came to Midnight Mass. One suicided in March. We had to break into his apartment in Darlinghurst to find him and the gun. The second man died of a heroin overdose in St. Canice's public toilets. I found him dead in the cubicle when I was locking up. The last man died of HIV/AIDS in the Sisters of Charity hospice in June.

After his mates died, the fourth man wanted to get out of King's Cross and start a new life. We helped him reestablish himself in rural New South Wales. I baptized him at St. Canice's in

1994. I did his wedding there in 2000. I received his wife into the Catholic Church in 2002, and the following year, at the only church they knew and liked, I baptized their triplets. Mark, the only Catholic on that first night at the church, now works full time with homeless teenagers in Sydney. He was once homeless himself, being ordered out of the family home at sixteen, when he told his parents that he thought he was gay. He and his partner remain devout parishioners of another inner-city Sydney Catholic parish.

Now, there are some Catholics and Christians who think that those "entertainment workers" should never have fronted up to Midnight Mass. They would most certainly believe that the Jesuits had no place ever going to *Les Girls* that night, of all nights, if any night. However, on both scores they are utterly wrong. The reason Christ and the Church touched these men's lives for the better was not just because they came to us, as good as that was, but that we got off our backsides and went to them where they were, and met them as they were.

In doing so, we formed a relationship with them that gave two of them options they and we could never have dreamed about for their lives that first night, and, at least for the other three, they received the dignity of a Christian burial, which I think is a dignity always worth having.

Our Christian belief should always connect our real lives with others so that we might be the best people we can be. At its best, it is never moralizing, but allows a tradition with ancient roots of reflecting on human nature for two thousand years and adapting it to the here and now. I find that liberating.

PART III

THE GOD OF LOVE
AND THE PROBLEM
OF EVIL

13.

BELIEF IN TIMES OF TRAGEDY

Without question, the biggest challenge to Christian faith is how a loving or good God can allow bad things to happen to good people. This problem is commonly called "theodicy" in philosophy and theology, where we consider the problem of evil while believing in a God of love.

Here my reflections come out of my experience grappling with a family tragedy, which forced me to confront some fundamental questions about my own belief in God. I don't want to claim too much for my work here. Over the centuries, greater minds than mine have applied themselves to these questions and have come to different conclusions. The problem is that when I most needed their insights, their answers were inadequate. To be fair, the vast majority of them did not have the benefit of contemporary biblical studies, theology, science, and psychology to guide them.

The Church knows, too, that it cannot be definitive about these matters, because, on this side of the grave, we just do not know where or how God fits in regard to the suffering of the world. Therefore I make no greater claim for my work than it has helped me hold on to faith in a loving God as I walked through the "valley of tears" and in the "shadow of death."

Let me begin with a story that explains why this question is anything but academic for me.

At dawn on the morning of my twenty-fifth birthday, the Jesuit superior of the house I was then in roused me from my bed to inform me that my mother was on the phone. I do not come from a very demonstrative family. We do not call each other at dawn on birthdays, but as soon as I heard Mom's voice, I knew this was not a happy birthday call. "Your sister has had a car accident and I have to get to Darwin immediately. I am hoping you might come with me." My sister, Tracey, had completed her nursing studies straight after school and within months was in Calcutta nursing at Kalighat Home for the Dying, Mother Teresa's first foundation. She had returned home after six months to care for my mother, who was not well, but later returned to India. Eighteen months later, the Indian government refused to renew her visa because she was a volunteer, so she returned to Australia and got a job working with the Sisters of Our Lady of the Sacred Heart in running a health center for Aboriginal people at what was then called Port Keats, but now goes by its traditional name, Wadeye. She was young, full of life, and very capable. She was enlivened by the community at Port Keats, as much as she had been by her work in India.

The day before my birthday, Tracey found herself relieving the local nurse in another outback town, Adelaide River, a small white and Aboriginal community about one hour south of Darwin, the capital city of the Northern Territory. What happens next is Tracey's story, so I will let her tell it from her book, *The Full Catastrophe*.

It is near the end of my time in Adelaide River that I drive over to Port Keats for the weekend. I take Margaret, the wife of the plumber, and her three children with me as her car won't be able to cope with the dirt roads. We have a wonderful weekend and are just outside Adelaide River on our return journey when the engine gives a cough and dies. Fortunately two vehicles come along shortly after we stop and they offer to give us a tow into town.

We are all hooked up and on our way, but before I realise what's happening I find myself driving over the tow rope with my car veering off to the left. I grip the steering wheel to cushion the impact of a small tree looming in front of me and the next thing I know, the entire car has rolled over, leaving me unsure whether I'm up or down. I cannot move a muscle and feel as if the entire roof of the car is pressing down on my head. My mouth and brain still work, though, and once I have ascertained the children are fine and Margaret is not badly hurt, I feel a great sense of relief. Our good Samaritans are in a great state of anxiety; one of them leans down to tell me that they'll go to Adelaide River and get the nurse. "I am the fucking nurse," I reply, and direct him to the house to which the regular nurse has just returned.

Many hours later and with police, ambulance and the nurse in attendance, I am freed from my metal entanglements. All I can feel is the most excruciating pain in my neck. They lay me on the ground, apply a neck brace, and then transfer me to a stretcher in the ambulance. One look at the worried faces of the people around me is enough to send my spirits plummeting. I have been conscious throughout this ordeal and my brain knows that I can't feel anything below my shoulders, but the rest of my body is resisting this information.

The trip to Darwin is agonisingly slow as the ambulance crew keep stopping every twenty minutes to check my vital signs. I threaten death if they stop the vehicle once more, as the pain in my neck with every stop and start movement is unbearable. My other great concern is a stabbing pain at the back of my head and a very real sensation that ants are biting my scalp. It takes a little time to convince the ambulance attendant that I'm not suffering from head injuries and am completely serious in my complaint. Determined to shut me up, she starts combing through my hair where, much to her surprise, she discovers several large green ants. The reason for the pain in the back of my head turns out to be a sharp piece of twig. We hasten to Darwin without further incident, and I lie back on the stretcher and hope that this is all some horrible nightmare.

I have the staff contact a friend of mine in Darwin to whom I entrust the job of ringing my mother and breaking the news.[1]

Jill rang my mother around 1:30 a.m. to inform her that Tracey had been in an accident, and while they were unaware of the extent of her injuries, Mother should come. Now, the next bit of the story is a "mother moment." (My mother was widowed when she was thirty-two. My father died of a massive stroke at the age of thirty-six, leaving my mother a single parent to my brother, who was seven, my sister who was five, and to me, who was only two.) Mom, who was living on her own at the time, decided that, rather than wake up Peter and me, it would be best that the two of us get a good night's sleep, because there was nothing any of us could do until dawn. Mom rang no one. She sat there drinking cups of coffee and smoking cigarettes until dawn.

By 9:00 a.m., Mom and I were on a plane to Darwin. If you have ever touched tragedy in your own life, you will empathize with the denial that both of us went into—we found everything on that plane journey hysterically funny. We both laughed that on arrival Tracey would be sitting up in bed, having a steak and a beer, laughing at us for being so melodramatic. Such a happy ending was not to be.

On our arrival at the airport, there were so many veiled and habited nuns I thought the pope must be arriving on the next plane. "The doctors will tell you everything when we get there." We were ushered in to where Tracey was and there was the long sheet, up to her chin. She had her arms extending out on boards at each side of the bed, and there were two huge spikes buried into her skull with weights at the back of the bed holding her head in place. I have never been able to look at a crucifix in the same way since.

My mother became very clinical and started asking Tracey what she could move. With two big tears just silently dropping down the side of her head, my sister simply said, "I'm a bloody quad, Mom. I have dislocated the fifth cervical vertebra and fractured the sixth and seventh vertebrae. This is as bad as it gets."

Now, the most common reaction to shock is either fight or flight, and we chose the latter. Tracey says that, between my mother and me, she does not know who beat whom to get out of the door first. The pastoral care sister put us in a room on our own. I sat at a desk and for one of the first times in my life, I was speechless. My mother started pacing the floor. She was angry. It was like one of the lioness's cubs had been left for dead and she was going to get whoever was responsible. As she paced, my mother started asking a series of questions:

"How could God do this Tracey?"

"How could God do this to us?"

"What more does God want from me in this life?"

And most hauntingly of all, "Where the hell is God?"

These were rhetorical questions, but being a Jesuit, God is my game. So I ventured an answer. It was the most painful and important theological discussion I will ever have in my life.

I told my mother that if anyone can prove to me that God sat in heaven last night and thought, "I need another quadriplegic, and Tracey will do, so let's set up a car accident to get that happening"—if this was God's active will, then I am leaving the priesthood, the Jesuits, and the Church. I don't know *that* God, I don't want to serve *that* God, and I don't want to be *that* God's representative in the world. So my mother came back at me, "So where is God then?" And I gently said that "I think God is as devastated as we are right now that a generous, selfless girl, who went all over the world looking after the poor, is now the poorest person we know." It had nothing to do with money. I did not have to choose between a God of love and a God who does cruel things to us. Like the God who groans with loss in Isaiah, and Jesus who weeps at his best friend's tomb in John 11, God was not standing outside our pain, but was our companion within it, holding us in his arms, sharing in our grief and pain.

In the months that followed, I got some of the most frightening letters from some of the best Christians I knew. I'm not blaming any of the writers for what they wrote. They offered what they thought was the best they could to give me comfort. It's just that what they said only ended up adding to my pain.

A few correspondents wrote, "Tracey must have done something to deeply offend God so God had seen fit to punish her in this life." They went on, "The only way to know peace with God, now, is to accept his will." They actually believed that God gets us.

I have discovered since 1988 that this theology is far more common than I would have ever imagined. I have met people with cancer, couples with fertility problems, and parents who have lost a child in death who have asked me what they ever did to deserve the curse under which they think God has placed them. I want to weep just thinking about them.

Others wrote, "Tracey's suffering is sending up glorious building blocks to heaven for her mansion there when she dies." This is what is usually called "pie-in-the-sky-when-you-die theology." I did not know that in heaven, in the many rooms of the Father's house, there are first, business, and economy class suites. And if that's so, then heaven will be the first counter in my life where I will not be looking for an upgrade! For if to get from the shanty town just inside the pearly gates to the best celestial suburb means being washed, fed, turned, toileted, and clothed every day for over twenty-seven years now, then I cannot pay the price for the move across town. I think very few people could.

Finally, there were scores of letters and cards that said, "Your family is really very blessed, because God only sends the biggest crosses to those who can bear them." I always like how some people who are not receiving that particular blessing can see it so clearly in other people's suffering. But let us think about this line a little more. We hear it often. If this line is true, then we should all be on our knees morning, noon, and night with only one prayer: "I am a wimp. I am a wimp. I am a wimp, O God. Do not consider me strong." Because if this theology were true and God thinks you are strong, you are going to be blessed with a big cross.

Added to these responses, good people, who were trying to be comforting, gave the usual trio of replies in the face of bad news: "It's all a mystery," "My ways are not your ways," and "Only in heaven will we find out God's plan." There is a truth in each of these statements, but I am not at all convinced that these bald statements are true in the way some people mean them. They are often used by good people to say something they hope will be comforting. It did not have that effect on me. For example, while it is absolutely true that God's ways and thoughts are infinitely greater than anything we can hope or imagine, invoking Isaiah 55 in the midst of people's suffering tends to place God outside our human drama, as an all-knowing and yet uncaring observer to the action of our lives. Yet I think one of the greatest points of the incarnation—of God becoming one with us in Jesus Christ—is precisely that God wants to reveal his ways and thoughts, wants to be known, especially in the moments when we are sometimes given to the greatest despair. Jesus, through his life, death, and resurrection, shows us that God has grafted himself onto human history in the most intimate of ways. We do not believe and love an aloof being that revels in mystery and goes AWOL when the action turns tough in our lives. The incarnation surely shows us that God is committed to being a participant in the human adventure in all its complexity and pain.

So I am very grateful to the correspondents who wrote to me after my sister's accident. They have alerted me to how often we hear some terrible theology that does not draw people to God in the worst moments of our lives. It alienates us. It alienated me for a while from believing in a God who wants us to have an intelligent discussion about the complexities of where and how the divine presence fits into our fragile and human world. So here are my six steps to spiritual sanity when we are tempted and give into the temptation to ask, "Where the hell is God?"

- God does not directly send pain, suffering, and disease. God does not punish us.
- God does not send accidents to teach us things, though we can learn from them.
- God does not will earthquakes, floods, droughts, or other natural disasters. Prayer asks God to change us to change the world.
- God's will is more in the big picture than in the small.
- God has created a world that is less than perfect (otherwise it would be heaven), in which suffering, disease, and pain are realities. Some of these we now create for ourselves and blame God.
- God does not kill us off.

14.

THE NATURE OF GOD

Tragically, I have come to see that some people believe in a tyrannical God. The usual modern idea about human tyrants is that they are absolute rulers who maintain their power through fear and death, torture and oppression. Understandably, most of the population do not take on the tyrant, not only because of their fear, but also because their primary task is *just* to try and survive the regime.

The people who wrote to me and suggested that my sister had to be punished by God for her offenses, or as a way to merit heaven, seem to believe in a tyrannical God. Tracey remains one of the finest and most generous people I know. The idea that life is about surviving the regime is much more alive and well in the popular imagination than we may like to accept. It shows its ugly head when we do or say something we should not have and then stub our toe. We can think that God is giving us an immediate wake-up call. This idea holds that God tolerates bad behavior up to a point, but then has to stop the nonsense by reminding us who is boss. Toes are one thing, quadriplegia is quite another.

This theology lurks behind those scandalous chain letters that masquerade as "prayer guides" to St. Jude, "hope of the hopeless," where, if we follow all their absurd instructions precisely, God will grant our petition. If our prayers are not answered, it follows we must have missed a step, and sometimes the chain letter says that any deviation from the prescription will be punished by God's wrath. Most of us do not take these things seriously, and nor should we, since it reduces God to the role of a ringmaster of the earthly circus, cracking the divine whip as we jump through the necessary hoops. And in the oddest contradictions, it can also mean that we believe that God will jump to and act in our favor when we fulfill the requirements of the chain letter. For the record, we do not have to write out a prayer nine times and leave it in nine churches, or forward nine emails, for God to listen to us or take our prayers seriously.

Some people say that the idea that God directly sends or wills pain, death, suffering, and disease is the "Old Testament image of God." While we all know there are parts of the Old Testament that reinforce such an image—babies' heads being bashed against the rocks, the enemy being smitten, and God killing off the firstborn sons of an entire nation—taken as a whole and with cultural intelligence and care, the Old Testament is a long and complex love song about salvation, and how God wants us to live, not die.

God as a tyrant is a fearful, neat solution to the deep pain within some people's lives. Suffering has to come from somewhere and when innocent people suffer, others conclude that the pain was sent directly by God. I use the word *directly* here very strongly. I believe that God has to take some responsibility for the moral and physical evil in the world, but only "indirectly." I imagine God could have set in motion a world that is better than this one, but I cannot be sure of that. Given that God wanted to give us the gift of free will—even to the point where we can reject God—and that, as a result of this freedom, we can make destructive choices, maybe this world is as good as it gets. In any case, we have to deal with the world as it is.

So I reject the idea that God is an absolute ruler who maintains power through fear and death, torture and oppression, primarily because I cannot see this in the person and work of Jesus, but also because I could not truly love such a God. Inverting St. John's words in 1 John 1, "true fear drives out love," I want to have "fear of the Lord" in its most traditional sense of being reverent before God, being in awe of God's presence and creation, but I also want to return the love of God with an offering of love. And to do so I cannot be frightened.

It would be impossible for any of us to truly love a God whom we honestly believed kills our babies, sends us breast cancer, makes us infertile, and sets up car accidents to even up the score. Even on its own terms, this God looks like a small god, a petty tyrant, who seems to be in need of anger management class, where he might learn how to channel that strong angry emotion into creation, not destruction. Furthermore, if God were into sending evil upon us, you might think he would start with the worst sinners, the real tyrants of our world, and leave the rest of us for later, but it never seems to go like that.

So how can I be so confident that God is not deadly by nature? First, we are told "that God is light and in him there is no darkness at all" (1 John 1:5). I do not want to be accused of "proof texting"—that unfortunate religious disease from which some Christians suffer, where they think a single scriptural text that seems to back up their argument is the last word on the topic. Taken in context, this verse is taken from a sermon about the light of God's love shining in and through Jesus. Probably written for the church at Ephesus in the latter part of the first century, it seems to be a rebuttal of a heresy that was present at the time and that claimed Jesus was more a spirit than one enfleshed. John is at pains to say that Jesus is God's light in the world in and through his sacrificial love for us, and that those of us who want to walk in this light must love others as Jesus loved us.

In this context, we can see how cancer, car accidents, and the death of children, husbands, and anyone we love are dark things that cannot have a place within God. They cannot be part of his arsenal of weapons to test us out, and to inflict pain on us to see how we cope. We are told repeatedly by Paul and other New Testament writers that death and destruction are manifestations of disorder, so they cannot be part of light itself, nor of pure love. The sort of thinking that suggests that darkness does in fact dwell in God has made its way into our ordinary conversation. Think of how many times we have heard a phrase like, "Well, that was the hand which I was dealt, so now I have to get on with it." Sometimes "the hand" being discussed includes the death of a loved one, growing up in a violent home, or suffering from a disease. The metaphor of life as a card game has its limitations in any case, but I am interested in knowing who Christians may think is the dealer when they use this phrase. In almost all cases, it is God, here seen to be actively throwing a roguish hand to unsuspecting and unfortunate players at life's table of chance. If we must use this metaphor, then at least we might be able to say that life is the dealer of the hand and that it is chancier than any of us might be prepared to contemplate. The good news is that, rather than see God in the dealer's seat, he is on our side, in every sense of that phrase, accompanying us with a complete stake in the game.

There is a huge difference between God permitting evil and God perpetrating such acts upon us. We need to stare down those who promote and support an image of God as a tyrant. In its place, let us cling to God, in whom there is no darkness, made visible in Christ Jesus, who subdues tyranny in all its forms and who not only accompanies us through pain, death, suffering, and disease, but even seeks us out when we are most lost, and guides us home.

GOD'S HOLINESS AND LOVE

The further element within the nature of God that we need to underline in this discussion is God's holiness and love; the God of Jesus Christ does not have an ugly, vengeful, and dark side. "God is love," St. John tells us. Love defines God's nature, was expressed in human form in Jesus, and is active in the ongoing action of the Spirit who inspires movements, choices, and works of love in us.

Therefore, the One God who must be unchanging or else we would never know where we stood, is not created by any other power or being, and is transcendent. This leads us to God's power and knowledge. I have no problem accepting that God is all-powerful and all-knowing. Indeed, we need God to be precisely that. There is no point having a God who is deficient in power and knowledge, for we might then want to trade in this God for another, later, and better model. The issue is not about God's ability to know and do, but how God's power and knowledge are exercised in regard to the world and in regard to us, and here the traditional arguments about God's knowledge or omniscience and his power are less attractive.

There are two ways of understanding what God might know and can do. The first is to accept that God does not know the unknowable and cannot do the undoable. In popular discussion, people will quickly reply to this thesis, "But God is God. He knows everything and can do anything." If this is true, then the unknowable is knowable—at least to God—and he chooses not to share it even with those who seemingly most need to know it, and the undoable is doable—at least to God—and he decides not to act, even though his inaction has such destructive results for the very people who believe in his presence and love. We have always believed that except for very rare interventions like the incarnation and the resurrection, God works within the boundaries of the principles governing the universe. We believe, for example, that God cannot make a square circle or build a building that cannot physically be built, so God's predictability entails respecting established boundaries.

Another way others have approached this issue is to hold that there are things God does not know and cannot do because God chooses it that way. I concede that this is a departure from traditional Christian doctrine of what God is like in his essence. But it seems to me that traditional theology has to trade away some of God's care and love and maybe even God's presence to hold on to God's power and knowledge, so let me give you a human example of how my idea might work.

At the risk of anthropomorphizing God, that is, making God in our image and likeness, my example is that of a parent of a teenager. A loving mother or father of a seventeen-year-old child may well want to shield their daughter or son from the potential pain and grief of the world by knowing everything that is happening in their child's life and by constantly intervening at the first hint of trouble. As loving and present as these parents might seem, chances are their son or daughter will be unprepared for adulthood due to well-intentioned but suffocating and controlling parents. They will have stunted growth. The reality is that, at least in Western society, there comes a point in a loving relationship between a parent and a teenage child when the parent has to let their children make their own decisions, not know everything there is to know, and stop intervening at the first sign of trouble. It can be frustrating and even heartbreaking for the parents, but the decision to limit parental knowledge and power does not come out of malice or because they do not care, but precisely the opposite, because they care enough to accept that the young adult needs the support and companionship of the parents while exploring his or her own world.

If this holds true for the best of loving parents in this world, why cannot it be true of our relationship with God? It has long been accepted in philosophy that God treats us like adults, that we are not God's marionettes, his playthings. Therefore, in dealing with us, in guiding us, in supporting us to achieve our full potential, God could know everything, but chooses not to, and could keep intervening, but chooses not to. These self-imposed limits on knowledge and power do not occur out of malice, but out of love for us and God's desire to see us grow.

15.

OUR SEARCH FOR MEANING

We do not need to blame God directly for causing our suffering for us to turn it around and harness it for good. The human search for meaning is a powerful instinct. Tracey's accident, however, was meaningless in itself. It was a random event, an intersection of the wrong time and the wrong place ending in the worst outcome. I say the worst outcome quite deliberately because, if on the day after the accident, when we arrived in Darwin, the doctors had said to us, "While you were flying here your daughter and sister died of her injuries, but we want you to know that had she lived she would have been a quadriplegic," we would have taken death as some sort of tragic comfort. In such a scenario, we may have been asking, "Who could ever imagine Tracey, of all people, being a quad?" or "How would she have coped?" and "How would we have coped?" It is these type of comments that I can imagine I would have said in the midst of my despair and grief.

So in some measure, Tracey turned around a meaningless accident and was generous with what she still had left to offer—her story, humor, wisdom, and experience. It was mostly out of sheer boredom, I think, but two years after her accident, Tracey decided to write up the stories of her life in Calcutta. Only a mother could have stored away in the loft every single aerogram that Tracey wrote from India over the years. They became the basis upon which she sat for hours hitting the keyboard with extensions on her two index fingers, weaving the stories into a longer narrative. It was slow work. By the end of that year, there were eleven pages to read. She sent them to me for feedback, "from your literary mates." One of my friends was the celebrated Australian novelist Thea Astley. Her brother, Philip, was a Jesuit. Thea may have been a sophisticated writer with Australia's highest literary awards to prove it, but her speech was direct and earthy. She rang me up and said, "Your sister is a bloody good storyteller, isn't she? She has the basis of decent book here." I put the two direct-spoken women in contact with each other, and they became firm friends, as I suspected they would. Computers have revolutionized disability, and within that year, Tracey had a voice-activated program to which she could dictate. With Thea's mentoring in the background, four years later, *The Full Catastrophe* was published, regaling the reader with stories of her life in Calcutta and the Northern Territory. Shortlisted in literary competitions that year for best new work, its biggest impact has been on adventurous young people, would-be volunteers, paraplegics, and other quadriplegics.

Through God's grace, the rest of us have learned a lot too about the big lessons in regard to ourselves, one another, and the precariousness of life. I have always been an incredibly active person all my life, but several years ago, one of my Jesuit superiors challenged me about my busy lifestyle. "Why are you on the move all the time?" he said. Without even thinking, I looked at him as my eyes welled up with tears and said, "Because I can."

One of the greatest learnings all my family has painfully acquired throughout this time is coping with the restrictions disabled people have to bear. I am the one who will confront you in the parking lot if I see you alight from your car with no disability sticker when it is taking up the parking spot for a person with a disability because it is the closest one to the shop. There are also hotels with disability bathrooms that no seriously disabled person could access. Our family has dined at expensive restaurants that charge my sister the same price for dining in their establishment where the only disabled access to the dining room was via the food lift with the cabbages and then through the pot wash in the kitchen. There are the cold temperatures of most public buildings, the way people yell in exaggerated voices at people they don't know in wheelchairs, presuming them to be mentally disabled and hearing impaired, as well as some contemporary architects who like to ward off skateboarders with cobbled pavements. Try going over those in a wheelchair.

Arguably, the most practical growth in the last three decades is gratitude for my bowel and bladder. I never thought the smallest room in the house would become a house of prayer. The old line runs, "You don't know what you've got until it's gone," and given Tracey's loss, I am now regularly grateful for the smallest things, for the fact that my bowel and bladder work and that I can go to the toilet on my own.

However the greatest gift this searing experience has given me is to have a greater empathy for anyone who is devastated in grief or who feels abandoned by life or God. I have touched that moment, and I have asked, on more than one occasion, "Where the hell is God?" That has irrevocably changed my ministry as a priest for the better.

Given that, with God's power and love, good can come out of disasters, this in no way changes the nature of the terrible event in the first place. It does not become God's will because we have grown as a result of a shocking event. If that were true, then it could be argued that because our study of genetics has benefited significantly from the evil experiments on 1,500 pairs of twins at the hands of the Nazi doctor Josef Mengele, then the good application of his findings to the later mapping of the human genome, and the cures that may come of this, means that God wanted these experiments to happen so that good would ultimately arise out of evil. I do not know anyone who argues this case in this way. In fact, there is understandable ethical disquiet in some sections of the scientific community about using experimental results acquired through evil circumstances.

However, this principle of revising the horror of terrible events in the face of later and good developments happens all the time on a more personal and domestic level. People will say, "Well, given all the good that has happened since, now I know why God took my husband or baby, or I got breast cancer or that accident occurred." Rather, I think spiritual sanity rests in seeing that in every moment of every day, God does what he did on Good Friday, not allowing evil, death, and destruction to have the last word, but ennobling humanity with an extraordinary resilience and, through the power of amazing grace, enabling us to make the most of even the worst situations and letting light and life have the last word. Easter Sunday is God's response to Good Friday: life out of death.

DIFFERENT TYPES OF EVIL

Philosophers have traditionally made helpful distinctions between different types of evil: physical, moral, and metaphysical, to name the big three. Physical evil is the one we have been considering so far, where even without an evil intention, unlike a murder, a bad thing happens to our person or living situation or personal and social freedom. Most people wonder where God is in physical evil; hence most of this book is on this topic.

Moral evil is the one we have probably heard about more than any other type. This is the evil that results from human choices and actions. In Christian theology, personal culpability for the moral evil I may choose, and social culpability too, hinges on how free, deliberate, and knowing I am in regard to the choices I make. This is where we talk of sin, informed conscience, and morality. There are overlaps between physical and moral evil, for while moral evil may have a very real physical outcome, the cause of it is not in the external world, which we cannot control, but in the process of human decision making that we can control.

Moral codes do not have to be religious. Every human group establishes boundaries for behavior, decision making, and punishment for knowing transgressors. All civil laws carry within them an agreed basic moral code, and many people who profess no religious faith have a highly developed secular and humanistic moral frame of reference within which they live their lives. The primary function of religion and morality is not simply to explain the how of living, but to place morality in the context of the why of it, and, indeed, the where of it: where we came from; why we are here, and where we are going. Religion is not about morality per se; rather, it provides for the believer meaning and coherence for why we live the way we do.

Metaphysical evil is about the clash of good and evil on a more cosmic level. This is the stuff of myth in its richest sense, where humanity tries to grapple with how evil started, whether this world is the best one that could have been created, and why God seems to permit suffering. The stories of Adam and Eve, the garden of Eden, and the fall, are the profoundest of myths, using simple stories to explain the bigger questions. An explanation of one type of evil begs questions in the other categories, as we will now see.

16.

THE ROLE OF PRAYER

There is no question that the Old and New Testaments and the Tradition of the Church urges persistent prayer for particular intentions, even for and against rain (cf. Jas 5:17–18). The problem is that these ideas emerge from a prescientific people, as we have seen, who thought that rain came from windows in the sky, which God opened and closed at will and whim. The dialogue between science and faith should also have an impact on the way we pray.

We often cast God in the role of the great meteorologist in the sky. Brides especially do this. I have lost count of how many brides over whose wedding ceremonies I have presided that have asked me to pray for a fine day. Except for the ease of the guests and the options a sunny day gives for a wedding photographer, I do not think it matters one iota whether there is hail, rain, or shine for a wedding or any other significant day. I think God has greater problems to worry about, at least I hope so. My anxiety is twofold here. Christianity has sometimes been critical of animist religions that hold elaborate ceremonies to get the gods of nature to do their bidding in relation to the weather. There is not much difference between the Hollywood cliché of a Chinook priest dancing around the totem pole asking the gods to "send rain, send rain, send rain," and a bishop having a "Mass for Rain" in his cathedral during a time of drought. The same theology can be active in both circumstances—if we pray hard enough or long enough or change our lives, God will relent and send the rain we need. My problem is this: What do we think God is doing in heaven? Is he sitting there saying, "No, I will not send rain, so go away, dry up, and die"? Surely not! I do accept that we might gather for a Mass where we ask God to make us strong in the face of drought. The Roman Missal has Masses for all sorts of desperate occasions. These can be easily reclaimed as part of a liturgical lament where we gather to cry out in our need to the same God who is already present to us, aware of our need, and weeping with us. The Psalmists were on to something powerful in this regard.

Certainly, we can and should pray about water, the earth, and the environment. If we are truly pro-life, it is inescapable that we have to be pro-planet as well. We might even have Masses where we ask for the grace to be the best stewards of creation that we can be, but this is a long way from the "Mass for Rain." This raises another vital point: What do we think we are doing when we enter into petitionary prayer—does prayer change God, change us, or change both?

God is not actively sending rain to increase my prayerful begging or to teach me to smarten up my act. By contrast, changes in the earth's climate may be due to a long-term cyclical pattern, which we have not had the tools to measure until now nor the records to read. Environmental disasters such as floods and droughts could be due to solar flares over which we have no control. Such disasters might also be the result of some countries populating the wrong areas, growing the wrong crops, and not being good stewards of the earth locally and globally. The worst case scenario is that such disasters are a combination of these factors. In any case, we now know that the earth is much more fragile than once thought, that it is more balanced and finely tuned. It is evolving all the time, now, literally, groaning in an act of giving birth. Every day it provides us with challenges about how we see ourselves as part of the created order, working with all living things in partnership for the future of the world given into our care. God accompanies us, guides us, and has instructed us about the consequences of greed and avarice and of not making better decisions, when the consequences of stupid ones, even in regard to weather and climate, are staring us in the face.

So if I should not pray about rain or a fine day for my wedding, then why should I pray at all?

A good number of Christians do not actually pray to the God

and Father of Jesus Christ, but to Zeus. Not that they are intending to pray to this pagan Greek god, but their approach to prayer leads me to conclude that some people believe in a Zeus-like god, and not just because he was Olympus's resident meteorologist.

In some circles, Zeus was mocked and challenged. So it was not as simple as a reward/punishment relationship, but it is true that, in the traditional presentation of Zeus in Greek mythology, he was a complex god to understand. Though he could be loving and kind, he was more famous for being moody and unpredictable. When his ire was raised, he killed, maimed, punished, and handed other gods and mortals over to be tortured in a variety of exotic ways. Life with Zeus was unpredictable.

Rightly, since the earliest centuries of the Church, our God has been different from the gods that had gone before—different from Zeus. Building on the foundation of Judaism, we proclaim that

God is one;
God is eternal: he will not burn out;
God is immutable: he does not change;
God is self-existent: he is not caused by any other being,
    he is the first cause;
God is transcendent: we are made in God's likeness, and
    not vice versa;
God is omnipotent: all-powerful;
God is omnipresent: all-present;
God is omniscient: all-knowing; and
God is holy: perfect in love.

Now some of these proclamations need unpacking, but before we do that, let's consider God's immutability.

The traditional Christian doctrine of immutability holds that God, in his essence, is unchanging. By the way some people speak of God, we get the impression that they think God could change if he wanted to because he is all-powerful. God's unchanging nature is essential for the sake of our relationship with him and our sanity. This affects petitionary prayer.

Now, our petitionary prayer tends to follow the categories of the psalms. Apart from asking God for something, our prayer can also lament our situation, that is, cry out in anguish; it can give thanks and praise; affirm our trust and faith; sing of our salvation; and simply wait upon the presence of God.

It must be conceded, however, that the most common form of address from humanity to God is asking for something to happen to someone somewhere. And yet, all the sacrifices and prayers in the world cannot change God because that is the way God wants it.

So what does our petitionary prayer do? Why bother praying to a God who does not change? When we pray, we are asking our holy, loving, and unchanging God to change us, and thereby change the world. Unlike Zeus, the real Christian God cannot wake up in a bad mood today, and he is not famously unpredictable. It is nearly impossible to have a steady and loving relationship with a volatile human being, so how much more fraught would our relationship with God be if he were characterized by being random (in the classic sense of the word) or erratic? Jesus, the Word of the Father for the world, was strong and constant. And on the nature of God, the Apostle James says, "Every generous act of giving, with every perfect gift, is from above, coming down from the Father of lights, with whom there is no variation or shadow due to change" (Jas 1:17).

This is a great relief in our life of faith and in our prayer. We do not have to be anxious about God's justified anger, at least in this life, and then fret about God killing, maiming, punishing, or torturing us. But you would be forgiven for thinking this after hearing how some people talk about God and how some of us were taught to pray. It seemed that prayer was all about asking—or telling—God what to do or to change his mind, like sending rain when he may not want to. The role of prayer is a serious part of our lives, so we should know who we are praying to and what we can expect from the encounter. If God cannot change from our prayer, we can, and we should.

Now, it may seem odd to claim that God cannot or does not change nature but can change the human heart. I do not believe, however, that God can change a human heart that does not want to change. Grace builds on nature; it does not obliterate it. We are seduced into changing by the grace of God, not forced to do it. There are enough examples of how good people make terrible choices and evil people do decent things for us to know that our freedom has been God's greatest and most risky gift to us.

A BIG-PICTURE GOD

I believe passionately in the will of God. It is just that the will of God is discovered on the larger canvas rather than in the fine details. I think God is a big picture kind of guy. Let me explain.

Going through Catholic schools for all of my education, we used to pray a lot about God's will. This was especially true when vocation directors turned up to ask if we were being called to the priesthood or the religious life. At these times, some people would be praying fervently, "Please, God, don't call me to be a priest"; "Don't make me become a nun"; "Do not send me off to be a brother." The way God's call was presented to us was, first, God called you, and if you heard or felt that call, you had to respond or else God would be very angry and you would be very unhappy, because, whatever you chose to do in life, it would not be what God called you to do primarily. In Catholic circles, this sort of thinking almost exclusively applied to vocations to ordained or professed ministry within the Church. Curiously, it never applied to the single or married vocation.

This approach to vocation is very limited. There is not much freedom for the respondent to respond. They are called and that's that, whether they like it or not. I have met priests and religious who live out of this paradigm. They did God a big favor by joining up, but they appear to have been desperately unhappy ever since. But since God called them, what else could they do? Unfortunately, they have projected their unhappiness on to countless numbers of children and adults among whom they have ministered, and the poor priests and fellow religious with whom they have lived. They really wanted to be somewhere else, doing something else, and being someone else. Having seen the havoc their vocation has wreaked, they really should do just that.

At a very deep level you have to want to be married to your spouse, live as a single person for life, or be a nun, brother, or priest. Saint Ignatius Loyola, the founder of the Jesuits, was very

keen on saying that God works in and through our desires, puri-
fied as they should be. If we do not actually desire the vocation
we are discerning, then we are going to be miserable, and I cannot
see how God rejoices at that fact or how we can be satisfied that
we made the best choice. Incredibly, I have met some outstanding
priests and religious, who say that they never wanted their vocations, would never have chosen it, but in fact their ministry has
proven that they are excellent at it. For whatever complex reason,
and paying every respect to them, they may be deluding themselves, and in the depth of their being, they want to be a religious
or a priest. They have chosen their paths.

Even in the story of the annunciation, Mary did not have to
say yes to the angel. Notwithstanding the grace of the immaculate
conception, if Mary did not have the power and freedom to say
no, then her yes does not mean very much. She would have been
God's victim, not the model she is for us of cooperating with God,
even when such a yes ended up costing her everything. Our yes to
grace sometimes does the same.

In the same vein, if a bride and groom do not freely and
knowingly choose each other, then the Church says that their marriage is invalid. The freedom to choose and knowing what we are
choosing, inasmuch as we can, is essential to the character of marriage. What fits for this call fits for all vocations in life. It may not
be easy. We may struggle with it. But the reality is that we have to
choose it, and in the process of discerning what we really want—
what we desire—we discover God's will. If we are forced or frightened of other alternatives, and indeed if we have no alternatives
at all, then we are not making a free and knowing choice; our
response is compromised.

On one level, therefore, I do not think God cares whether
I am a Jesuit or a priest. I think God wants me to live out the
theological virtues of faith, hope, and love (1 Cor 13). This call
is not just for me, but for all God's children everywhere; that is
why an inescapable dimension of our faith in God is to work for
justice. We can glimpse the establishment of the reign of God in
this world, as well as in the next, by creating a community where
all people can realize their potential to live lives worthy of their
calling to be faithful, hopeful, and loving. There is not a heavenly
blueprint, as such, for my life. Through the blessing of time and

place, the gifts of nature and grace, I work with God to realize my potential in the greatest way possible, even if that involves having to do things that are difficult, demanding, and sacrificial. This response is not out of fear and compulsion, but comes from love and desire.

The greatest test for the proponents of God's will as a blueprint for each individual life, and indeed for every living thing, is not found in most of our lives, but in the lives of the poorest of the poor. Whatever of my angst over what I might choose with God's grace to do with my life—what about a child who dies from malnutrition hours after being born? Or the twenty-eight-week-old fetus who, in some countries, can now be legally aborted? And the list could go on and on. Are any of these tragic situations God's active, specific will for these sisters and brothers of ours?

On a more mundane level, we sometimes hear people say after they narrowly missed being involved in an accident, "But for the grace of God, it could have been me involved in that misfortune." In other words, it was not God's will that I was involved, this time. Here, my problem is not that someone avoided being in an accident, but what we are saying about the poor people who were involved. It would seem that we are saying that it was God's will that they be involved in the calamity. Mind you, I recall the story of the elderly Jesuit priest who was nearly run over by a car one afternoon. That night, as he was recounting his near miss to his Jesuit community, he concluded his triumphant tale by saying without irony or insight, "But for the grace of God, I would be in heaven tonight."

The way we imagine the nature of God, then, determines how we consider God's will. If we believe in Zeus, then we have to do all sorts of things all the time to keep him on our side. If we see God as the divine tyrant, then not doing the tyrant's specific will ends in grief in this world and the next. He knows everything, even the unknowable, and so what we have to do is find out what he knows about our future and do it. This sort of theology is operative in the story of the Jesuit priest who fell off his bicycle and broke his collarbone. The bone needed pinning, and as he was preparing for surgery, a religious sister brought him holy communion. After she gave it to him, the sister said, "Father, it is obviously God's will that you slow down and have a really good rest." The Jesuit replied, "If that's true, Sister, I'm pleased that God didn't think I needed a sabbatical."

Given that faith, hope, and love mark out God's will in the big picture, and that God and I have to work out the details together, then the task of discernment comes into its own. For now, I want to introduce a person who has assisted many, many people in discerning where and how God is working in their lives, and in how to discern their next best choice in the light of faith.

17.

ST. IGNATIUS LOYOLA (1491–1556)

They say a Jesuit cannot give a talk or write a book without mentioning Ignatius. Well, here he is—and he matters when it comes to avoiding evil and choosing the good.

Name changes are significant in the Bible. The most famous ones in the Old Testament are Abram to Abraham, Sarai to Sarah, and Jacob to Israel. In the New Testament, only two people have name changes: Simon to Peter, and Saul to Paul. They indicate a turning around of one's life after a commissioning by God. Some Catholic religious men and most religious women used to take on the name of a patron saint when they entered religious life as a mark of the change in their life. Since 1009, almost all popes, on being elected into office, have done it too, though John XII (955–64), Benedict IX (1032–48), Boniface VIII (1294–1303), Clement VI (1342–52), Sixtus IV (1471–84), Innocent VIII (1484–92), Alexander VI (1492–1503), Julius II (1503–13), and Julius III (1550–55) should not have bothered with the name change, because the only difference we can find in their behavior was that each one became demonstrably worse afterward.

Now, St. Ignatius of Loyola was born in the Basque region of northern Spain in 1491. We know from family records that he was baptized Iñigo Lopez de Oñaz y Loyola after St. Enecus (Innicus), abbot of Oña. He changed his name himself, in Paris around forty-one years later, to Ignatius in honor of the early martyr, St. Ignatius of Antioch. His name change represents an extraordinary journey that he was both completing and upon which he was embarking: from soldier to saint, from philanderer to founder, and from masochist to mystic.

Does the first part of the last category sound harsh? I may be the only Jesuit who will tell you this, but St. Ignatius was also an obsessive, compulsive, neurotic nut. That's not fair, of course, because he was also a genuinely holy, mystical, and brilliant man of his time, but some of his behavior can easily lead us to conclude that my comment is neither facetious nor unwarranted. In fact, one of the most important chapters in his life gives the key to why Ignatian spirituality has been so enduring and adaptable. Contemplate the cave at Manresa in 1522, where Ignatius had his best and worst days. Ignatius dictated an autobiography, and we know from it and from letters he later wrote that it was in that cave that his "Rules for the Discernment of Spirits," arguably his greatest gift to the Church, was formed. That cave was also the scene of some very dangerous behavior.

We know that, on the way to the Benedictine abbey located on the mountain of Montserrat, from where he left for Manresa, he encountered a Muslim man who defamed the Virgin Mary. Iñigo was so offended he wanted to kill him, but he could not decide whether or not to do it. Just ahead there was a fork in the road, so he loosened the reins on his donkey. If the donkey chose to go the same way as the Muslim, he would murder him; if it took the other path, he would not. Thank God the donkey had more sense than Iñigo! In the cave, we know that Ignatius, the penitent, whipped himself three times a day for months, wore an iron girdle, fasted on bread and water for which he begged, slept very little and only then on the ground, spent up to seven hours on his knees at prayer, covered his face with dirt, grew his hair and beard rough, and allowed his dirty nails to grow to a grotesque length. We also know that he suffered so badly from spiritual scruples that he considered committing suicide by throwing himself into the River Cardoner. These days, we would diagnose the Ignatius of 1522 as being an at-risk self-harmer suffering from an acute depressive disorder and exhibiting suicidal behavior.

Two things saved him. First, because he was a soldier, he was used to taking orders from legitimate authorities and following them. Second, he believed in the wisdom of the Church. When his Dominican confessor at Manresa saw how far Ignatius was deteriorating mentally and spiritually, he ordered him, under holy obedience, to eat food, wash, cut his hair and nails, stop the penances, and take care of himself. Ignatius had to obey. From there, Ignatius turned a corner and emerged a wise and holy man. Manresa changed him forever, not just because he had undergone these terrible experiences and lived to tell the tale, but because he reflected carefully on how good things like prayer, penance, and fasting can quickly become instruments of self-destruction, even in the name of God.

The life of Ignatius appeals to anyone who has glimpsed a very dark place and has needed to find a way back from that abyss. His wisdom in regard to the careful discernment of spirits was won by staring down some very destructive demons indeed. Most importantly, the insights of Ignatius are practical. In modern parlance, we would now say that Ignatius encourages us to "keep it real."

Ignatius says the spiritual quest starts with our desires, asking, "What do I really want in my life?" Our desires are pivotal to our search. We often look for all the right things in all the wrong places, and some pay for it for the rest of their lives. Unlike what many people think today, Ignatius would not rate "being happy" as the most important desire to have and possess. Not that he was against joy. He was certainly not a member of the fun police. In fact, Ignatius was famous for his sense of humor and he loved a party. It is just that he would argue against what we sometimes hear parents say they want for their children: "I don't care what my kids do, as long as they're happy," or we might say, "I need to make some big changes in my life because I should be happier." Maybe we need to make some big changes in our life, but not for the primary pursuit of happiness. In this world, everlasting happiness is a myth. Ignatius knew that.

The social researcher Hugh Mackay sums up our contemporary problem with enshrining happiness as the essential human goal:

> Weekends should be great....Holidays should be havens
> of happiness....Work should be fun, or, if not fun, then

at least stimulating and satisfying. So should marriage, and if it isn't, then we should strive for a perfect divorce in which we and our former partner will behave in the civilised and responsible way we couldn't quite manage during the marriage….The kids themselves should be gifted in ways that make them worthy of special attention….Our counsellors, it goes without saying, should be gurus….Sex should be blissful and deeply satisfying, every time….Sport? It's all about winning, of course….Our cars should be perfectly safe….The state should leave us alone to get on with our lives in peace but should exert tight control over the behaviour of other people who mightn't be as responsible or competent as we are….In our perfect world, blame is easy to affix, revenge is sweet, and outcomes are always positive (for us). Life should proceed from one thrilling gratification to the next, banners triumphantly aflutter, joy unbounded. All we want is heaven on earth. Is that too much to ask?[2]

When he emerged from the darkness of that cave, Ignatius knew that happiness would be the welcome by-product of living out the highest goals in life: to be the most loving, hopeful, and faithful person possible. How would people respond if we were to make that response our new mantra to the question of what we most wanted for our kids. "I really just want them to be the most faithful, hopeful, and loving people they can be." As in everything important in their lives, our children and young adults would learn what this looks like from the adult role models around them.

For the last thirty-two years of his life, Ignatius embodied Jesus' call to love God, his neighbor, and himself. He knew that learning from hard-won lessons, confronting tough moments, and embracing suffering were inescapable and important moments in coming to grips with our human condition. He also knew that, when we try to do this on our own, we can be defeated by isolation and fear. That is why he put such store in the community of faith, the Church, because he knew we needed each other and that God was found in the midst of companionship, of being "friends in the Lord."

St. Ignatius Loyola (1491–1556)

Consequently, Ignatius thought the task of life was to be as reflective as possible—"a contemplative in action"—so as to discern the patterns that lead us to be more hopeful, loving, and faithful, as well as to learn those patterns that lead us to being less so. Ignatius knew that most positive and negative things in our life don't just happen. He believed very strongly in habits, in building on the good ones and working against the bad. This means constantly assessing the "what and why" of our decisions.

Ignatius also knew that, before we come to make a decision, we need to address the three big blocks in most people's lives that can blind us from a range of choices: riches, pride, and honor. From his own experience and in accompanying many others in their spiritual search, he knew that these vices entrapped people.

Riches are not just about money, but the enticement of material wealth as well as physical beauty, intellectual prowess, reputation, status, and power. It all centered on who possessed whom or what. Ignatius was once incredibly vain in the pursuit of worldly wealth and status for its own sake. It was a dead end for him and he suggests it is for all of us. He also argued that riches lead to honor, where we want to be acclaimed and praised all the time, and we expect that life will be easier because of our wealth and power. This is not new. Seneca, a second-century philosopher, noted in his book on anger how the richest people he knew also seemed to be the angriest because they thought their money would buy them an easier life in every way. When it didn't, they became angry. Furthermore, riches and honor lead to pride, where we have to be like God—always in charge. Today, we would call proud people, in the sense that Ignatius uses the term, control freaks, trying to control everyone and everything for their benefit or to their will. For Ignatius, the spiritual quest is about staring down the seductive side of these things and reclaiming wealth, beauty, status, intellect, and power as gifts given by God to be used for the coming of Christ's kingdom. Note that he did not reject these elements in our lives. He was smarter than that. He recrafts them for higher and better purposes.

Ignatius thought that in the spiritual life there are three types of people: the first is the one who lives from desire to desire, not caring about God one way or another; the second is the person who wants to attend to their spiritual journey but their bad habits, negative attitudes, and vanity get in the road of making much progress; the last type is the one whose genuine desire is to follow God and live a life of faith, hope, and love. Rather than a type of person, each is a stage, through which we all too often move in and out, and backward and forward.

To keep the momentum going in the right direction, Ignatius encourages us to deepen our humility. The spiritual concept of humility has had a bad rap. It does not mean feeling bad about oneself. The word comes from the Latin *humus*, meaning "close to the earth," and a good way to start being truly humble is to fight against a sense of entitlement and simply be grateful for everything. We did not create the world; we inherited it and, as a start, that should make us profoundly grateful. Keeping it real! Ignatius presented three degrees of humility: the first degree is found in a person who lives a good life so as to attain heaven; the second degree is a person who lives a good life in order to bring faith, hope, and love to bear in our world in a way that liberates others as it has liberated them; finally, there are those who want to be like Christ in every way, serving the poor and being a prophet, and prepared to take rejection and insults so as to point to a greater love.

There is great symbolism in a name change. Ignatius went from being a vain, violent, but aimless egotist to knowing that the desire to be a faithful, hopeful, and loving follower of Christ was the best way to live. His conversion is enshrined in his "Prayer for Generosity":

> Take hold of me Lord.
> Accept this offering of freedom, of memory, of mind,
>   of will.
> These I cling and count as my own.
> All are your gifts, Lord, now I return them.
> They are yours. Do as you will.
> Give me only your free gift of love.
> In this you give all; in this you give all.[3]

All of this is important background to understanding the very real and stark human experiences that gave birth to his profound insight into how we read the action of God in our lives.

DISCERNMENT OF SPIRITS

From reading St. Ignatius on discernment in his *Spiritual Exercises*, his letters, and other writings, I have compiled twelve contemporary spins on his timeless wisdom about how to minimize evil in our lives and world by the choices we make:

1. Trust the common place, the ordinary, the everyday. Live in the here and now. Sometimes we live in an unhealed past or an unknown future, whereas God may be found right under our nose, here and now. The good spirit draws us to deal with our ordinary life, as it is, not as we may like it to be, and there discern his presence. We often look for God in the spectacular and extraordinary, yet he is to be found in quiet and mundane moments. He comes to us poor, naked, in prison, hungry, and thirsty. We need to be wary of false consolation. "The good can be the enemy of the better." We are both attacked at the most vulnerable parts of ourselves, and allured by the narcotics of modern living—drugs, alcohol, sex, work, gambling, technology, and shopping—which never take away the pain of living but temporarily mask its effects.

2. Do not make a decision when we are down; allow the crisis to pass. Sometimes we make the worst decisions when we are under pressure. It is always better to let a crisis pass and then in calmer surroundings weigh up all our options.

3. Be suspicious of "the urgent." Sometimes we have to make a big decision quickly. Buying some time, any time, is always helpful for working out the best course of action. The good spirit brings a sense of perspective and priority to problems. We need to be especially careful in making a life-changing decision that goes against another life choice made properly in a time of consolation, in peace.

4. Be humble enough to take wise advice. We are not meant to be "rocks and islands," operating on our

own. We need the wisdom of our families and most trusted friends, the Church, and sometimes professionals to inform our consciences and make the best possible decisions before God. Remember that the word *obedience* comes from the Latin word *obedire*, meaning "to listen." If we all want to be obedient to God's reign in our world and lives, we had better get good at listening, in all its forms, because we believe that God listens to and hears us.

5. There are always patterns to the action of the good and bad spirit in our lives. Sometimes we think something "came out of nowhere." Sometimes it does, but most times the good and bad that beset us have a history and a context. We have to train ourselves to read the signs of both, cultivate the things that are good and see the empty promises of the bad spirit and how it leads us into dead ends. A daily examination of conscience helps us to see the pattern of the Holy Spirit.

6. The signs of the good spirit are courage and strength, consolation, inspiration, and peace, feeling as though obstacles can be overcome, and that we are worth something and can contribute good things to the world. Saint Paul also provides a helpful list in Galatian 5:22–23: "The fruit of the Spirit is love, joy, peace, patience, kindness, generosity, faithfulness, gentleness, and self-control." The signs of the bad spirit are sadness, obstacles that seem insurmountable, lack of self-worth, turmoil, impulsiveness, negativity, agitations, and regularly giving into temptations.

7. A good or better decision is just one decision away. The bad spirit always convinces us we are trapped and there is no way out, diminishing our memory so we keep repeating destructive behavior, even though it never helps, it alienates us, and does not help us deal with our situation. A journal, wherein we review our life and its patterns with compassion and courage, can help. For more important discernments of our heart, mind, and soul, we can draw up a list on one side of

the page with the movements for A, the movements
for B, the movements against A, and the movements
against B. The process does not focus on which list is
the longest, but where our heart and head are drawn.

8. The good spirit connects and frees us to bring out into
the open anything we keep buried in the dark. The
bad spirit divides, isolates, and locks us in our fears.
Every time we are transparent with those we love and
trust, the good spirit is at work. There is nothing we
have ever done, are doing, or will do that will stop
God from loving us. There is nothing that God cannot
forgive and heal, but we have to start with owning up
to ourselves and what we have done. Then, anything
and everything is possible.

9. The Holy Spirit is always present where a community
of faith in God gathers. In the community, we discover
that we are not the only ones who have ever had to
make a particular choice or that we are not the first to
face similar problems.

10. Get our heads and hearts in dialogue; we need both.
Some believers think that Christian faith is cerebral.
While theology has a venerable intellectual tradition,
and thinking clearly is very important, our heads have
to be in touch with our affective lives and our instincts.
When our head and heart are more integrated, we have
a good chance of putting our hands and feet in a place
where we will do the greatest good for the greatest
number. Our head can be filled with dreams, some
of them good. Our heart and gut can hold desires.
Which dreams and desires persist? Which ones lose
their appeal over time? What are our deepest desires?

11. No work for the coming of the kingdom is too small,
irrelevant, or inconsequential. We can often be
conned into thinking that our relatively small and
daily acts of kindness do not count for much in the
spiritual scheme of things. Wrong! If there were more
evil actions than loving actions in our world on any
one day, the earth would be unliveable. Simple and
selfless acts of kindness might go unreported, but

they change the world by enabling Christ's love to break through into the world of our daily lives.

12. Fidelity is one of the greatest gifts of the Spirit. Even in the face of opposition and other choices, remaining faithful is a heroic act of love. That said, the gospel calls us to "die unto self," not to "kill self." It is never God's will, for example, for a person to stay in a physically, emotional, and spiritually violent relationship. Ignatius encourages us to imagine we are advising our best friend about the matter we are discerning. What would your counsel be? Alternatively, imagine being on your deathbed. What choices do you wish you had made or not made as you review your life? Hopefully, these choices have made you more loving, faithful, and hopeful.

Discerning from a position of being in love is superbly sum-marized in one of my favorite quotes attributed to the former Superior General of the Jesuits, Pedro Arrupe, SJ:

Nothing is more practical than finding God, that is, than falling in love in a quite absolute, final way. What you are in love with, what seizes your imagination, will affect everything. It will decide what will get you out of bed in the morning, what you do with your evenings, how you spend your weekends, what you read, who you know, what breaks your heart, and what amazes you with joy and gratitude. Fall in love, stay in love, and it will decide everything.

18.

FREE WILL AND THE PROBLEM OF EVIL

Earlier we noted that philosophers and theologians regularly make a distinction between different types of evil: moral, physical, and metaphysical. These distinctions rightly matter in academic circles, but they count for less to the person in the street. Evil exists and God has at least permitted it all to happen. There has always been overlap between these categories, and never as much as now. With the help of science and the media, we are starting to see the extent of the impact of our lives on one another and the created world. There are still some people, often atheists, who say, "You all believe in a God of love, and yet there are famines and wars. I will believe in your God when these things stop." While I acknowledge that God has to take some responsibility for the world as it is, for now I want to deal with the overlap between moral and physical evil. Starvation is the most confronting example.

Every time there is another famine in the world, someone says, "How could God let that happen?" It's impossible to have absolutely reliable figures but, despite the fact that we live in a world where we could feed everyone, UNICEF estimates that sixteen thousand children die each day from starvation. That means eleven children die every minute of every day. So in this context, we can see how moral evil moves over to physical evil, and not just in the sense of weather. Most famines are not solely caused any more by droughts or floods. The Food and Agriculture Organization says that general poverty, lack of democracy, civil war, and unjust access to world markets are as much to blame for starvation as climatic factors, if not more so now. So, when people say, "Why does God let famine and starvation happen?" I imagine God shaking his head in a tearful reply, "Why do you let famine and starvation happen?" In most of the wealthy countries of the world, elections are fought on economics, but the people who have the least rarely rate a mention. When was the last time that any of us can remember a candidate who was or was not elected because of their stand on Third World development? When did we last hear a significant stump speech or a campaign debate about what any of the political parties are going to do for the 80 percent of the world's population who will not vote in our elections, but whose life and death may be in part destined by it? When did we ask our elected officials for his or her policy in regard to intervening to stop general poverty, lack of democracy, civil war, and unjust access to world markets for all God's children?

God becomes a convenient whipping boy in this debate, but the ball is squarely in our court. In a world where all people could be fed, why do people starve? We choose it to be this way. Indeed, some frustrated economists who work in this area go as far as to say the G20 needs it this way and structures the global market accordingly. Whatever the details, the evil here is ours, and God will call us to account for it. And because of access to the many forms of media, we will not be able to say to God that we did not know either the scale of the problem or our complicity within it. Ignorance cannot be our defense. The same is true of other examples as well: environmental degradation, personal and social stress, and lack of action to end war. We choose the world to be like this, and then blame God for the negative fallout from our decisions.

Nevertheless, it remains true that God must take some responsibility for the world in which we live. He permits evil things to take place. As I have said earlier, I am not given much to speculation about whether this is the best possible world or not. It is the world we have and so I accept it as the place wherein we exercise our free will, as the best world we can have. By virtue of our choices, we can improve upon it, or leave it impoverished. Some people speak about the world in such terms that leads me to conclude that they want it to be perfect. In Christian theology, at least, this would mean it would be heaven, so we have to accept that anything less than heaven allows for the possibility of a world that is less than prefect. In this less-than-perfect place, then, we exercise our free will, which, as we know from personal and social experience, can be a mixed blessing in what it bestows on us, others, and the world. Free will is such a critical gift for humanity that to give it with one hand and then create a perfect world within which to exercise it with the other would result in never seeing the fruit of our good choices or the destructiveness of our poor ones. This now leads me to consider God's power, or more precisely how God might exercise that power in the world.

Traditional theology holds that God is one, does not change, is not caused by any other being, is transcendent, all-powerful, all-knowing, all-present, and is holy or all-loving. I accept all these things, but the last two I want to cling to for dear life in any discussion about evil.

If God goes to sleep or takes vacations from the world—as some Jewish theologians argue must have happened between 1939 and 1945—then we are really in trouble. It means the world goes into free fall for a while. This could explain how on October 23, 1998, God dozed off at the wheel of the world, while my sister was alert at the wheel of her car. I cannot imagine that to be true, for God would seem to be lazy or negligent. God is always present to us as a companion in the vicissitudes of life and death. This is what the Christian doctrine of the incarnation is all about. God so wants to be in relationship with us, so that we might be loved and saved from evil and ourselves, that he became one with us in our flesh. Christianity is the only world religion to assert this extraordinary truth.

19.

WHAT OF MIRACLES?

That miracles occur seems to be beyond dispute, especially in the realm of physical, emotional, or spiritual healing. In classic Christian dogma, the believer is required to affirm that miracles happen, and that the author of the miracle is God. I can affirm both easily. Like many fellow Christian travelers, I also share a healthy interest and belief in miracles. I do not, however, believe that they come from without. I believe God works miracles from within. I have no concept of God "zapping" people with miraculous power. Such an idea can reduce God to a magician, gaining the admiration of the spellbound audience, who longs to see his next amazing trick. One of the many problems with this model is that the most deserving people, like my sister, never seem to be called up onto the celestial stage. I also reject this "magic model" because I cannot find it in the actions of Jesus. "Sign faith" in John's Gospel was considered the weakest faith of all. If miracles were simply a question of God's power, then why did Jesus not perform miracles always and everywhere? The Gospel writers often put it down to a "lack of faith," which already allows for other preconditions for a miracle to occur.

Contemporary neuroscience is just starting to understand the general properties of the brain and the organ's potential to heal. I think miracles occur when some of these healing properties are released by the brain into the body. For some, the reception of the anointing of the sick and the laying on of hands unlock these properties. For others, it may be a pilgrimage to a holy place, personal or

intercessory prayer, devotion to a saint, and for more secular people who have experienced a miracle, it may be a complete change
in lifestyle, diet, and the practice of meditation. This understanding may explain why Jesus could perform some miracles and not
others, and why, at Bethsaida, Jesus had to have a second go at
healing the man born blind. Even an encounter with Jesus or a
single touch was not enough for some people, while for others
their master's or friend's desires to see them well was enough to
effect the change. Given that Christians readily concede that the
evolution of the human brain is among God's greatest handiwork,
then God is, in every sense, the author of the miraculous. It is a
question of where God's grace resides. It is not just from without.
Brian Doyle captures the same sense:

> We think of grace arriving like an ambulance, a just-in-
> time delivery, an invisible divine cavalry cresting a hill
> of troubles, a bolt of jazz from the glittering horn of the
> creator, but maybe it lives in us and is activated by ill-
> ness of the spirit. Maybe we're loaded with grace. Maybe
> we're stuffed with the stuff.[4]

Miracles do happen, but the writers of the film *Bruce Almighty*
were inspired when they placed these words on the lips of God:
"Parting your soup is not a miracle Bruce, it's a magic trick. A single mom who's working two jobs, and still finds time to take her
son to soccer practice, that's a miracle. A teenager who says 'no' to
drugs and 'yes' to an education, that's a miracle. People want me
to do everything for them. What they don't realize is they have the
power. You want to see a miracle, son? Be the miracle."[5]

The challenge, then, is to read the sign of the times in our
imperfect world in such a way that responsibility is apportioned
properly. There is plenty of it to go around. God is responsible
for allowing a world to evolve within which the effects of moral
and physical evil can create injustices. But God is not responsible
because we refuse to make the hard choices that would transform
our world into a more just and equal place for everyone. In the
face of this obstinacy, it is not surprising that we seek a divine
scapegoat to carry the guilt for our lack of political will and social
solidarity.

20.

GOD OUR FRIEND

When I go near a nursing home, I am regularly asked, "Father, why won't God take Nana?" To which I reply, "Because Grandma hasn't stopped breathing yet." I don't actually say this. I have more pastoral sense than that, but I want to. Using the cricket or baseball metaphor, we can say, "Well, Gran has had a good inning." This works well enough when the person who has died is at an advanced age. The same line and its grateful sense breaks down completely when I am with parents who have just lost a child at any age, but especially at a still birth or when a child dies during its infancy. No parent should ever have to bury their child.

Raw grief is felt when a child is seriously ill or after he or she has died. In the face of this tragedy, Christians have sometimes said, "God must have needed another angel in heaven."

I know well-educated parents who have walked away from the practice of their faith because no one was able to help them think through a more coherent meaning to the life and death of their children, other than to say, "We will find out in heaven, when God will wipe away all our tears." While this may be true and there is a mysterious dimension to all suffering, saying that death is a mystery does not let us off the hook from using our intelligence and reason to speculate about some better answers. And while some of these responses may not answer all the questions we have, they might be more comforting than the banalities that currently pass for words of Christian comfort.

For the record, God doesn't need angels in heaven. In theology, we say that God is sufficient. God does not need anything, and therefore he has no need to take our children from us in any way, shape, or form—angelic or otherwise. What is exciting about Christian faith is that we believe God wants us. That is why humanity was created. It is possible to argue that God wants some human beings so much that God takes them back to heaven quickly, prematurely by our standards. Many sincere Christians believe this, but it is a very hard line to run in the face of a parent's loss. The tyrannical God, whose desires can ruin our lives, returns. I have no problem about the journey motif common in so much of our funeral language these days, but I steer well away from talking about God "taking us" or "calling us" in and through death; it is unhelpful in the way it can compromise God's love and goodness. Why would God's desire "to take" a two-year-old to heaven be more than God's desire "to leave" this child in the arms of loving parents? And if God is into taking and calling the children we love in death, then why not include those who are physically and sexually abused from the youngest ages by their evil parents and families, or who are orphans standing up in their cribs with outstretched arms and no one to cuddle, love, or adopt them?

In contrast, it is entirely appropriate to believe that life, from the womb to the nursing home, is not allotted a span, as such, by God, but that our body will live until it can no longer function, for whatever natural or accidental reason. God is not an active player in this process, but, again, has to take responsibility for making us mortal. In classical theology, the alternative would have been for us to have been created a disembodied spirit or an angel. But then I would not be me.

Traditionally, we have said that what survives human death is our soul or spirit. I have come to the opinion that whatever else might characterize the soul, memory is an integral part of it. Our memories survive us.

This is why I do not believe that God kills us off, but as painful as death is, we know that we will see our brother or sister again, and that Christian hope says that our parting is not a definitive "goodbye," but more a "see you later."

Some might think that the theology outlined here presents God as remote, aloof, or uninvolved. I don't have to believe that God has to be the direct cause of everything in my life to have a strong and lively belief in a personal God. Indeed, I am passionate about God's personal love and presence being present in the drama of our living and dying.

God accompanies us at every moment of our short or long life. The word *accompany* here is a strong one. It can mean to attend actively to someone, to be concomitant, to add and enrich, and to support (as in a musical accompaniment). Each meaning adds a layer of depth regarding how God accompanies us in life and through death. I also like the fact that the word *accompany* is a Middle French corruption of the words *companion* and *company*, which are from the Latin words *cum*, "with," and *panis*, "bread"— with one who breaks the same bread. This has all the sense of solidarity that "we are in it together," which defines Christian hope. God is in this with us, which is, of course, the story of the incarnation.

This image is appealing because we choose our friends and they choose us, we like to spend time with them, and we tell intimate things to our best friends that we tell few others. Sometimes, when we are on top of the world or in a crisis, we may call our best friends even ahead of our families. And we know our friends like us because they seek us out and want to share our life. They accompany us throughout life, attending to us, and enriching and supporting us. We experience friendship especially at meals, while breaking the same bread.

It is not childish to call God our friend, or to claim Jesus or the Spirit as our best friends. I think it is a particularly adult idea. Jesus is with us at every moment of life, especially when we wonder where the hell God has gone. Like all our friends who truly love us, God does not inflict pain, set out to punish us, or set up accidents to teach us lessons or make us grow. Although this unchanging, divine friend may be eternal, self-existent, transcendent, holy, and ever-present, God's love knows restraint, as the best love always does: a self-imposed restraint on his power and knowledge. Therefore God does not send natural disasters or famines. God does not kill us off. In fact, this heavenly friend wants nothing to do with death. We know that because of what we see in Jesus. In him there is no darkness, only light, no retribution or revenge, no smiting of the enemy. There is a demand for justice but no reprisals. And Jesus did not enter our world to die but to live, and to be our Way,

Truth, and Life. Just as Jesus was killed because of the way he lived, so too, God's last word on Jesus' death was life, to raise his Son from the grave. As a result, this friend's will or plan for us is for us to flourish in faith, hope, and love as we realize all our gifts and talents.

Yet Christ-as-friend does not barge in. He waits patiently for an invitation to enter our lives at whatever level we want. Jesus meets us where we are, embraces us and holds us close when the going gets tough, and helps us find the way forward, even on that last day when we find the way home.

21.

LOVE IN TRUTH AND ACTION

Since writing *Where the Hell Is God?* and because many people went on to read Tracey's *The Full Catastrophe*, I have been inundated with inquiries about how my family has fared in recent years. Given that the unforeseen journey of three of my recent books started with my reflections on my sister's car accident, it seems like a perfect conclusion to this part of this book to return to them, because they do in fact inspire me to be more faithful, hopeful, and loving. But I do so tentatively because recently my sister said to me, "It's time you gave up on our family for material and work on your fellow Jesuits." She is right. They have been the source of some of the most humorous and most serious moments in my life. It was also from them that I learned how to tell a story.

My brother, Peter, says that he is the forgotten member in our family. Many people who have heard Tracey's story know about Mom and me, and then, on hearing about Peter, they say, "I didn't know you had a brother." That would be music to his ears. Peter is also the most normal member of the family: Tracey is a nurse and now a quadriplegic; I am a Jesuit and a priest. Peter, however, owns his own very successful business and has been married to Michelle for over thirty years. They have three wonderful children and two marvelous grandsons. Peter is four years older than me and very different. He was always a natural sportsman. I was good at books, debating, drama, and music. I was a huge disappointment to him growing up. He gave up on me one day when I was playing football. When I got the ball and saw all the other boys, who were much larger than me, running toward me, I ran the wrong way and threw up the ball at the other end of the field, allowing the opposition to score. Happily, it was the end of my football career. Peter had to leave the sportsground, and I went back to the choir.

It was only as adults—after Peter got married to Michelle—that we got to know and like each other. By then, he was over getting me into the backyard and toughening me up! However, of all the causes for admiration I have for him, the greatest is that for the last twenty-seven years, he has been so faithful in his devotion to the care of our sister. Even when he had small children waiting at home, it was a rare day he would not quickly call in to check if Tracey and our mother needed anything done. Equally generous has been Michelle, who to my certain knowledge has never once complained about Peter making that detour home. Many other wives and mothers of young children to be bathed and fed would have had an angry moment. Not Michelle. They have been a generous and loving team to all of us, models of quiet unassuming support and love. Peter is a humble man in every best way.

Tracey has been a quadriplegic for over twenty-eight years. Though she had some understandably rocky days early on, she is one of the most emotionally even people I have ever met. She is almost always good natured, interested in the world around her, and encouraging. I have lost count of the number of people who have only met Tracey through her or my writings, yet who ask how she is. They feel a genuine connection to her. People have told me that Tracey's moving book *The Full Catastrophe* had such an impact on them that, since reading it, when they are having difficult days, they think of her and it helps to put their own problems into perspective. I do exactly the same, but not only because contemplating quadriplegia snaps me back into gratitude for what I have, but also because Tracey's good humor in the face of daily trials challenges me. If she can wake up and get on with the day in good cheer, then I sure as hell can too.

My mother was married eight years when, at the age of thirty-two, she became a widow. Dad was thirty-six. He had a massive stroke. I was actually with Mom when she found out about Dad's death. I was two months shy of my third birthday. My father owned a stock and station agency in Warwick, Australia. It was the first Tuesday in August 1966—Dad's day to go to the local sale yards and auctioneer sheep and cattle. There were some clients who would have no one but my father as their auctioneer.

He had woken up that day with a headache, which he did not describe in any different terms other than that. My mother, a nurse, had given him some aspirin and told him if it got worse to see the doctor later in the day. Dad was actually in the ring auctioneering when he collapsed and died. In a small country town, where my father was a notable and much-loved local figure, word spread like wildfire. At the time Dad died, Mom and I were at a department store in the main street of our town. As we returned to the car from the store, an unknown lady approached my mother, visibly shaken, and through her tears, blurted out, "I am so very, very sorry." Mom thought the woman was terribly confused or nuts, but it was an unsettling experience, so rather than continue on shopping, we went home. As she drove into the driveway of our house, waiting for Mom at the front door was the priest and Dad's best friend.

I grew up, therefore, in a single-parent family. Can we please stop giving all single parents a hard time? Some are certainly negligent and their children suffer. Many others, however, are heroic in the way they raise their children. Though a classic family home with a loving father, mother, and children is always to be preferred, children of single-parent families are not always going to be deprived of the essentials and grow up to be deficient adults. My mother raised her children as best she could, and then, at the age of fifty-six, when we became adults, she became the primary caregiver for her quadriplegic daughter. Now in her eighties, my mother gets up twice a night and turns Tracey from one side to another. She has been doing that almost every night for the last twenty-eight years.

Saint John reminds us, "Let us love, not in word or speech, but in truth and action" (1 John 3:18) and later, "Let us love one another, because love is from God" (1 John 4:7). In the practical, daily, and loving actions my family have shown each other, I have seen God in action, and have been inspired to be worthy of such an example.

PART IV

LIFETIME LESSONS
ON PRAYER

22.

WHAT IS PRAYER?

If God exists and if our God is a God of love, even in the face of pain and suffering, then what does prayer do? Why pray at all, and how do we know if it is achieving anything? Before discussing how we pray, we need to consider the multiple contexts within which we do it. If our prayer is to encounter God's presence, then we need to begin with our own situation. While God already knows my situation, it helps to become aware of what I bring to prayer, how I am feeling, and what obstacles might stand in the road of good communication today. Taking this excellent principle from the particular situation to the more general context, owning the wider background against which I pray, and the obstacles therein, makes the process a little easier to understand.

To illustrate this process, let me tell you about the person who taught me more about prayer and its importance than anyone else.

DOING YOUR BEST

I never knew Helen Leane by her baptismal name. Until I was an adult, I did not even know she had a baptismal name. She was Sister Mary Consuelo to me, a Sister of Mercy in the order founded by the Venerable Catherine McAuley. She was my first-grade teacher. In the preface, I shared that one of the distinct groups of interlocutors I meet on planes is those educated by nuns, brothers, or priests who did not experience a happy time of it. This group is now often made up of lapsed, collapsed, or ex-Catholics, and on long-range flights, I have to hear about their tale of woe in regard to Sister Mary Agapanthus. While some of these horror stories are true, I don't share them because, while I was a little overawed by the nuns, the ones I knew were mostly loving and kind.

In fact, the best thing to come out of the Vatican's investigation of religious women in the United States has been the general outpouring of affection by the former pupils and present admirers of nuns. I am not on my own in believing that some of the finest Christians I have ever been honored to meet are women in Catholic religious life.

Sister Mary Consuelo was five feet tall and four feet wide. Behind her back we called her Sister Mary-Consume-a-Whalelo. She was firm and fair. She needed to be. She once told me that in the forty-four years of her teaching career, she never had less than forty children in her class. In 1959, she had sixty-one children in the same room. There were forty-two children in my first-grade class in 1969. Can you imagine that ratio now? In the first grade, Sister prepared us for our first confession, as it was then called, and our first holy communion. I remember being so terrified going into the dark box to make my first confession, that when the slide pulled back, I could barely see through the grill. In my anxiety, I started yelling on top note, "Bless me, Father, for I have sinned. This is my first confession and these are my sins." At that point, the dean of the cathedral said, "God's not deaf and neither am I!"

I wish I could say that I was really looking forward to my first holy communion because I wanted to receive the Lord in a special and unique way. But that would be a lie. Actually I was terrified of doing something wrong during the Mass and of biting the host. At the age of seven, what I was really looking forward to was the party that followed the Mass and the presents I would receive. Back at school on the day after my communion, Sister Mary Consuelo asked me what gift I enjoyed the most. Of all the Bibles, holy pictures, rosaries, and medals I received, the gift I treasured most was a bone china holy water font of the Madonna and Child. "I would like to see that," Sister Mary Consuelo said. "Would you bring it to school tomorrow?"

The next day, during the first break—little lunch we used to call it—Sister was on playground duty. She was wearing a large blue and white striped apron over her habit. Imagine this scene. There were over seven hundred children in my Catholic primary school, and there was only one teacher supervising all of us—a ratio of 1:700. That would be illegal today. Not that Sister Mary-Consume-a-Whalelo had any trouble controlling the masses. She was a formidable figure who was as wide as she was tall, and ruled the playground with a whistle. Do you remember how big the nun's pockets were in those habits? Seemingly, the nuns carried everything in them, and they could put their hands on what they needed at a moment's notice. I raced up to Sister, who was surrounded by children: "I've brought the holy water font, Sister." "Very good, go and get it." All wrapped up in tissue paper, I carefully took the font out of my bag and then ran down to the asphalt playground. I was so excited at showing off my favorite present that, right in front of Sister, I tripped and down I went. The font hit the asphalt too. It did not break. No, it smashed into tiny pieces. Sister swung into action. She was an old hand at health and safety, long before the term was invented. Into her pocket she went. Out came the whistle and with a full, shrill blast seven hundred children froze on their spot. Sister said to the children in our vicinity, "Whoever picks up the most pieces of china will get a holy picture." We thought that was something back then.

The second whistle rang out, and while 650 children resumed their games, fifty children did a forensic search of the area, picking up every piece the naked eye could see and dropping them in the hammock that Sister had made from her apron with her left arm. Meanwhile, in my distress, Consuelo's right arm brought me in for a very big hug. Sister had many gifts, but among them was a very ample bosom. In fact, whenever we read about God's deep and consoling breasts in Isaiah 66:11, I go back to grade one. With one action, I was enveloped in her very ample bosom. I couldn't breathe and I wasn't sure I was ever going to get out of there alive. In fact, I think I made my decision to become a celibate priest at that moment.

When the bell rang, I was released from her profound embrace, and Sister rolled up the apron and walked me back to class. Three weeks later, she told me to stay in at little lunch. I thought I was in trouble. When every other child had left the room, she opened the drawer of her desk and there, wrapped up in new tissue paper, was a fully restored holy water font. By then, I think I had forgotten about it.

In those days, we knew very little about the sisters; they went to Mass, said their prayers, and taught school. Before Sister Mary Consuelo became a nun, however, Helen Leane had done a degree in fine art, majoring in watercolors and ceramics. She had taken those hundreds of fragments and spent hours and hours piecing back together my holy water font. When it was set, she repainted the entire object. The only sign that it had ever been broken was the rough plaster of Paris on the back. She could have thrown those pieces away and I would have gotten over it. In fact, I had. However, such was the effect of her prayer life on her relationships, even with a seven-year-old boy: she spent what must have been most of her leisure time for weeks reconstructing a treasured gift. But she was the real gift that day, and it was the best lesson I had from her.

While not an overly sentimental person when it comes to things, and having been privileged to have studied or worked in Australia, the United Kingdom, Italy, and the United States, nevertheless, everywhere I go to live, that font goes too. Soon after being ordained a priest in December 1993, I was honored to be asked to preside at the Eucharist at Emmaus, the Sisters of Mercy nursing home in Brisbane. Sitting in her usual spot in the front row was Sister Mary Consuelo, now age ninety. As part of my homily, I told the other hundred sisters the story of the holy water font. When I was done and sat down, Sister got up from her place and turned around to the others and said, "I told you I was good!" She was very good indeed.

I visited her when I could over the next few years. My last visit with her was in early March 1996. At that time, she knew she was dying. She talked about it openly and calmly. I asked her if she was frightened to die. "Oh no," she quickly retorted, "I'm frightened of pain, but I am not fearful of death because I have been praying all my life, preparing for that final journey home when I hope to meet Christ face-to-face, and hopefully hear him say, 'Well done, good and faithful servant—with what you had you did your best.'" As I drove away from her that final day, there was Helen in my rear vision mirror, now a frail wizened figure waving goodbye. I had tears streaming down my face in gratitude for a teacher who never stopped teaching, an adult who simply and appropriately loved kids who were not her own, and a believer who showed me that prayer is about living this life as fully as we can so that when we come to die it's an opportunity to hear Christ say, "With what you had you did your best." If that's what prayer does, bring it on!

23.

WHEN PRAYER IS PERSONAL

The first context within which we pray is personal. Some of us make a fundamental error by confusing private faith and personal faith. They are very different realities. The faith Jesus lived and invited us to share was about assisting him in building the kingdom here on earth, as it is in heaven. While we must have vital, important private moments in our prayer, Christianity involves our personal faith being enacted in the world around us.

If our personal prayer is an encounter, rather than going through motions, then religious experience is what gives our prayer its foundation, its heart. Without a religious experience, prayer is like throwing words on the other side of the wall hoping that someone's there. The constant repetition of formulas and rituals, even when these are ancient and beautiful, end up being an act of the will and mind more than an affair of the heart and a movement of the emotions. An encounter, no matter how big or small, is the wellspring of personal faith in God.

Friedrich Schleiermacher, William James, and Rudolph Otto gave us a theoretical structure for how personal mystical experience—the immediate consciousness of the Deity—fits into the communal one. Otto's famous dictum regarding religious experience is the *mysterium tremendum et fascinas*—the mysterious encounter that is both frightening or overwhelming and fascinating at the same time. I am happy to concede that the appeal to religious experience must itself be contextualized, that my religious encounters, my prayer, are of God, my belief in God, and of the community who nurtures my faith.

THE PERSONAL IS SOCIAL

The other context in which we pray is social. On that score, religious experiences and prayer in Western society have never had less support. We need to acknowledge at the outset of this discussion that there are those who dispute the reality of my personal religious experince, and dismiss it and all religious experiences and any belief in God as manifestations or symptoms of a psychiatric disorder. One neuropsychiatrist argues that religious faith is part aberrant perception and part belief pathology. In *Evolution and Cognition*, Ryan McKay claims that religious experiences can be put down to "individuals…(who) tend to be misled by untrustworthy sources of information, and/or tend to be prone to having their belief formation systems derailed and overridden by their motives (wish fulfilment being chief among them). Motives thus help to explain what maintains delusory beliefs once they have been generated by first factor sources."[1]

There are, however, several other scholars, including some who have no religious affiliations and who began their investigations not believing in the truth of religious experience, prayer, and mystical claims, who have ended up, not uncritically, accepting that the phenomena was real. Joseph Marechal in *Studies in the Psychology of the Mystics*, Louis Dupre in *The Other Dimension*, and Jacques Maritain in *The Degrees of Knowledge* fit into this category. The reality is that if prayer, religious experience, and mysticism are symptoms of a psychiatric pathology, then it is the most multilayered, multicultural, and crossgenerational pathology ever. I concede it's possible.

Even in difficult social contexts, however, God's love is not just about God loving me. Prayer is generative; it is making space for God to love us, and for God to invite us to have the courage to return the compliment, through the community of faith. It changes lives.

IMAGES OF GOD

There are so many images of God in the Old and New Testaments that entire books have been written on this topic. Some of our evangelical brothers and sisters have gone through the Bible and have compiled a list of over 230 names or images that are used for God.[2]

For many Catholic, among the best impacts of Vatican II have been the many and varied biblical images of Father, Son, and Spirit that replaced the rather stern policeman and judge that many people had for a long time. Today, some people in the Church either cannot understand the fear that motivated many people in their faith, or else they argue that it is overstated.

When we stand before God with the weakness and sinfulness of our own life, God will not settle old scores, nor take revenge, nor exact retribution. Rather, God will be perfectly just and completely compassionate. How can I be so confident? Because that is the way Jesus acted with those he met, and this is the overwhelming picture he paints of his Father in heaven in the Gospels. Whatever image we find helpful in our prayer, we do not believe in a nasty God in heaven with the loving Jesus who came on earth, and the emboldening Spirit who abides with us still. We believe that to have seen the Son is to have seen the Father and the Spirit. They are one God and act accordingly.

I am always consoled, for example, that the most ancient image of Jesus used by the earliest Christians in their art was that of the Good Shepherd: a gentle, protective guide who seeks out and saves the lost one. When in the catacombs, we might expect to find crucifixion scenes everywhere, but we don't. We find Jesus as a young shepherd boy, holding the sheep on his shoulders leading it home. As powerful an image as Jesus on the cross is for us now, it was not until after Christianity became the imperial religion in the fourth century that images of the crucifixion became popular. No doubt, that image emerged so strongly at that time because the cross went from being a scandal, folly, and a stumbling block (1 Cor 1:1) to becoming a sign of the one who was crucified but is now also the emperor's God.

In the Scriptures, there are three different categories of images for God:

- a political leader: king, lawgiver, judge, and warrior;
- someone who is part of day-to-day life: a father, mother, potter, a homemaker, doctor, shepherd, friend, lover, a woman about to give birth, gardener, and healer; and
- an aspect of nature: light, breath, a rock, the mountaintop, clouds, fire, a shield, bear, lion, or eagle.

At various times and stages of our lives, different images will mean more to us than others. There are plenty to go around.

An image that has come to mean more to me in recent years is the Father, Son, and Spirit as homemakers. The image of God as homemaker is, sadly, not very developed in Christian spirituality, maybe because too many undomesticated men have had too much say for far too long! But this is an image that is significant in how and where we meet God in prayer. My old professor of liturgy used to say, "A priest who cannot host a dinner party well should not preside at the Eucharist." You can see where this is going, and why. Jesus was good at dinner parties as host and guest. Meals mattered, and they still do.

In John's Gospel, Jesus says that as a result of our love for him and our fidelity to his word, the Father will come and make a home with us. The best homes are places where we relax because we are ourselves, we are known, and we know the others with whom we live. There is something intimate and familiar about our home that enables us to relax on many levels as we turn the key. Home is an earthy place where we don't get away with much and our vulnerability can be on display. A home, however, is more than a house in which people live. Homes need work and attention. A friend of mine says memories rarely "just happen"; they need to be created. That's the sort of attention to a family's life that turns a house into a home. And this is the world in which God enters our lives. God wants us to be relaxed and vulnerable in his presence. We don't need to put on a show or say what we think God wants to hear—that's a theater where we perform, not a home where we know each other. One element of our prayer is being comfortable and intimate, being who we are, rather than the persona we would prefer God to see. As with most of our homes, being at home with God has its ups and downs: some days when we think we cannot bear to stay one more moment, other days where we could never imagine being anywhere else, and then most days where we are neither up nor down and we just get on with the routine of our lives. What I find compelling about this image is that in prayer God the homemaker seeks me out in the room where I have taken refuge that day and draws me out to enter the fray.

Without question, the most invoked image of God in prayer is as Father. We do it every time we say the Lord's Prayer. And so we should. For though it was not the only name Jesus used for God, and only one of the many images upon which he drew, it is a privileged name and image.

We have been given both a vivid imagination and a vast array of biblical images to help us pray in tough times. For whatever image or word we use, God is always more than we can ever say; but that does not mean our names are unimportant, for our image of God reveals our personal theology as well. God meets us where and how we are, and not where we might prefer to be.

CHRISTIAN PRAYER

If we need rich and varied images for God for our prayer, we also need many ways of praying. We don't have to invent these, for they are already in the Scriptures and our Tradition. We simply need to remind ourselves of them, maybe be introduced to them, and adapt them for the here and now. Christian prayer has followed the categories of the psalms. Here, and elsewhere, are the different categories of prayer based on them:

- praise and thanksgiving;
- lamentation, crying out in anguish;
- affirming our trust and faith;
- singing of our salvation; and
- waiting upon the presence of God.

PRAISE AND THANKSGIVING

Naturally, with age and maturity, we are grateful for different things. Since my sister's car accident, which rendered her a quadriplegic, I am especially grateful for the seemingly small things of everyday life, the earthy things I can do but she cannot. Don't say this book isn't practical, because if you have never sat on the toilet and been filled with praise and thanksgiving because you can go all on your own, then your prayer life is about to become a lot richer. The old line goes, "You never know what ya got until it's gone." I often turn the smallest room in the house into a house of prayer.

I work often with teachers and one thing that has struck me in recent years is how many of them say, "The fastest disappearing words in the English language are *please* and *thank you* because these days, kids think everything is a right." We should not just blame parents and their children for this. Have you noticed that common courtesy is on the wane and how angrily demanding of everyone around them some adults seem to be? I am often embarrassed at how people speak to those who are serving them. Good customer service should not come because I yell louder than everyone else. We are better than that.

The reality is that we all need to cultivate a habit of saying "please" and "thank you," not just because it is a sign of a civil society, but because it enables us to recognize that each person has human dignity and deserves our respect, even if they are being paid to do their job. It helps create a world in which people are never mistaken for commodities.

It is not by accident that praise and thanksgiving are linked in the Psalms. The people I know who are most grateful are also the most generous when it comes to praising others. Often the people we find hardest to praise are those to whom we are closest, our wife or husband, children, friends, parents, or members of religious communities. We don't have to be stingy with praise; there will always be enough to go around. We just have to make sure it is sincere. There are those who worry that these days, when no child can fail and everyone wins a prize, our children are not as emotionally robust as they need to be to suffer the disappointments of life. There is something in that, but we don't have to withhold praise from one another, we just have to find opportunities to truly and authentically celebrate what we can.

If we are full of praise and gratitude for the daily things and the people that enrich our lives, then larger moments of recognition and appreciation take care of themselves. A good place to start is to write down all the things for which you are grateful. It does not matter how small or seemingly stupid they are. It's your list. In compiling that list you are already praying, because an ancient cornerstone of prayer is that our desire to thank God is itself God's gift. Be grateful.

LAMENTATION, CRYING OUT IN ANGUISH

Earlier, when I was advocating that we should not pray for rain, I went on to suggest that rather than gathering for a Mass to ask God to open the heavens, we should gather in a church for a liturgical lament, a collective expression of communal pain, crying to God about how we are experiencing our present life, and inviting God into the griefs and anxieties of the moment. In Catholic liturgy, we have lost the power of lamentation. The Psalmists had no such problem. They cry, they scream, they demand, and they rail against God over their pain. By comparison, our liturgical behavior is very tame—at least in the Christian West.

In our spiritual or physical rooms, some of us have no trouble lamenting our situation. Not that everyone can. Many people have told me that, while they would like to yell at God, they cannot. I remind them that of the 150 psalms, sixty-five are categorized as cries of lament, anger, protest, despair, and complaint. I send them off to pray over Psalm 88, the darkest of all the psalms, and then encourage them to go on to Psalms 3, 12, 22, 44, 57, 80, and 139. Not that I share in any way the belief in some of these psalms that God has sent the misfortune in an active way, but I am in awe of the way the Psalmist unloads on God. It is consoling and terrific. Such confidence!

God has big shoulders. He understands our lamentations because he knows the anguish in our hearts. I think God lives by the generally sensible advice: better out than in. We should all bother him a lot more with all our lamentations. God can take it.

AFFIRMING OUR TRUST AND FAITH

There has been a lot of research about how one person trusts another. It hinges on being vulnerable to the other. This is easier when it is between human beings and we can see each other. We cannot see God, only feel and encounter him, so being vulnerable to God is not easy. To accomplish this trust, we need that most subtle of gifts, true humility. If we want our prayer to be about trusting God, we have to stop trying to be the Creator and be the creature. An AA slogan sums it up nicely: "Let go and let God."

Other things that assist this trust are the mutuality of the relationship—when both parties are prepared to take appropriate personal risks, and there is an inability to control the other person. In each case, we can see how this works out in our relationship with God. Out of love, God gave us life and invites us, rather than coerces us, to respond to that gift in a mutual exchange. God has taken great risks in creating the world and giving us free will. Along with St. Paul, we can affirm that God risked everything in taking flesh of our flesh in Jesus and offering us salvation. Regardless, when we enter into a relationship with Christ, he enables us to take the risk of not living half a life, but of realizing our full potential and living life to the full. While some think trusting God means we have to become God's marionettes, the relationship into which we are invited is much more about a mutual and respectful relationship. It has long been accepted in philosophy that God treats us like adults, that we are not God's playthings. In fact, the opposite is true. In giving us free will, God does not want to control us, but waits patiently, inviting us, alluring us into a life of grace.

The Jesuits and Dominicans have been fighting over who controls whom and for what reason since 1588. It is called the debate over free will and grace and it became highlighted with one question: "Could Mary have said no! to the angel?" The Jesuit position was that Mary could have said no to the angel, but what makes her yes richer and stronger is the gift of human freedom. The Dominican position was that, due to the grace of the immaculate conception, Mary had to say yes to the angel. In 1597, Pope Clement VIII established the Congregatio de Auxiliis to settle the theological controversy between the Dominican Order and the Jesuits concerning the respective role of grace and free will. Although the debate tended toward grace, the pope encouraged both sides and the controversy was never clearly resolved. (Of course, the Jesuits are right!)

If we have the humility to let go and let God, it does not mean that God does all the work. It means that in our prayer, God treats us as adult, in a mutual relationship where, with God, we are invited to risk things, maybe everything.

Trust in God is often about being vulnerable to God through the seemingly ordinary events of life and responding in the most generous, good, and loving way possible.

SINGING OF OUR SALVATION

The repetition of prayer isn't just about doing the same dumb things over and over. It is the practice of attuning our hearing to listen to the sound of God's voice so that, even if it is faintly heard amid the din, we pick it out, lift our head, turn our gaze, and walk toward it. These days, there are a multitude of voices clamoring for our attention, and the loudest or the longest ones are often not the wisest ones. There are many songs we can choose to sing. We need practice at listening, hearing, attuning our ears, and adding harmony.

The psalms are replete with invitations to sing of our salvation. Psalms 95, 118, 62, 20, and 13 are just a few of them. Singing commits things to memory in ways that the words on their own do not.

Maybe this traditional category of prayer is not actually about singing—as good as that is—but rather a metaphor about words and memory. One of the finest themes to emerge from the Old and New Testaments is that of remembrance. The Jews are constantly told to commit this to memory, not to forget what God has done, and to keep calling it to mind. Jesus says to celebrate the Eucharist "in memory of me," and even the good thief simply asks Jesus to "remember me" when he comes into his kingdom. The word *remember* comes from the Latin *rememorari*, "again" and "be mindful of," literally "recall to mind." The reason we are constantly told to remember is, as poet and philosopher George Santayana states, "Those who cannot remember the past are condemned to repeat it."[3]

Taking the Bible as seriously as we should, the worst thing to forget is what God has already done for us. We have been saved in Jesus Christ the Lord. We don't save ourselves. We cannot earn salvation by good works or prayers or penance—our responses to the salvation of Christ that we claim here and now. And how we live is the way in which those we love will find the gift of God's salvation for themselves. Now, we all know we are a work in progress. We may well be saved by Christ, but it is quite another thing to accept that gift, claim it, nurture it, and live it in our daily lives. We can freely reject it. Some do it every time it's offered. We sing of God's salvation so that we remember not only what help has been given in ages past, but what help and companionship is available from God right now.

We also sing about what will be in the future. To learn this saving song, to sing it well, to understand its nuances and possibilities, we need practice and repetition so that, at the moment of our death, in the midst of all the other sounds as we leave this world, we will hear Christ's voice: soothing, reassuring, comforting, and confident. And it's our prayer that as we hear God's merciful and loving song, we will do what we have tried to do throughout our lives—recognize it clearly, savor it, walk straight toward it, and join in the chorus—because it will be singing our song.

WAITING UPON THE PRESENCE OF GOD

In the Scriptures, we are called "to wait upon the Lord" 106 times. Psalms 25, 27, 37, 52, 62, 104, 106, and 130 all call us to wait, in the sense of being patient. You can't rush God. Using the modern vernacular, this means that some part of our prayer life should be about "chilling out."

This idea of waiting in our prayer may seem to be passive, but it can also be a very active business indeed. In Hebrew, the word for *wait* is *qavah*, which means "to bind together into a cord." It comes from people understanding that while a piece of string might be strong, when you bind the strings together into a rope it can be immeasurably stronger and more workable. So when we wait upon the Lord in prayer, it can be about harnessing our resources, doing a stress test, and making sure that all our energies are pulling together in the same direction in loving and serving the Lord each day.

The most common time to "wait upon the Lord," however, is when we are anxious. Think of people waiting in hospital corridors for news of a sick relative, or a parent who stays up with an infant who may be teething or has a high temperature. Some sit by the phone waiting to be reassured that a loved one is safe and well, or that we have passed the exam or have been offered the job. Many of us have sat in a doctor's clinic waiting for a medical result. Many of these occasions are highly stressed. These can be the hardest moments in which to pray. But we have a great patron saint in Simeon, the old man who waited and waited because he believed the Lord's promise that he would not see death without seeing the Messiah. This tender story is stunning just as it is, but giving it a more psychological reading, we can see that some things cannot and will not go in peace until their time has come. We can't force them. Earlier, I noted that we cannot save ourselves. As difficult as this is to hear, it is equally true that we cannot save anyone else. That includes our children, spouse, grandchildren, parents, or friends. Sometimes we pray because there is nothing else we can do. We don't have to get the words right or even know the details of how we want something to develop, we just want the one we love to be at peace, made well, free from fear, and to be more faithful, hopeful, or loving. My favorite verse at times like this is, "The Spirit helps us in our weakness; for we do not know how to pray as we ought, but that very Spirit intercedes with sighs too deep for words" (Rom 8:26).

Following my sister's car accident, I revisited the emotions of that moment many times: no words; no great ideas; just numbness and powerlessness. It was when the pain was most acute that I started lighting candles in churches again. I thought I had left that pious practice behind in childhood. How wrong I was. As much as I understand the fire codes that govern churches' insurance policies these days, I feel let down when a church does not have a shrine at which I can light a candle. I also resent those flickering electric utilitarian contraptions. They exude no poetry. Rather, in a time of anxiety when we are waiting for a better dawn in regard to a particular dark night, there is nothing as satisfying as taking a small candle, lighting it, seeing it among scores, if not hundreds, of others, and leaving it there with my prayer as we wait upon the Lord.

It doesn't matter if we have developed bad habits in limiting prayer to only asking for things, but prayer is much, much richer. By all means continue to ask God to keep changing us, but let's also give praise and thanksgiving; cry out in lamentation; affirm our trust and faith; sing of our salvation; and simply wait upon the Lord. There is a way to pray for all seasons under the sun.

24.

WHEN PRAYER IS PUBLIC

Except under extraordinary circumstances, Christians not only have public faith, but they also gather with other Christians to pray, especially on the Lord's Day.

Liturgies in all their styles and forms are not about the power of a larger number calling on a changeable God to roll over on a particular point. That would be a political rally. No, liturgy is where we join our personal prayer with the prayer of the assembled Church, the whole people of God, asking God to change us so that we might more reflect his loving face and thereby transform the world.

Indeed, in *The Catechism of the Catholic Church* (nos. 1068; 1136–40), the Church says that liturgy is primarily an action of Christ, who gathers the whole community of the baptized to enter into full, conscious, and active participation in celebrations so that the faithful might go out and bear witness to Christ in the world. This is a pastoral issue today. There are now an increasingly unchurched number of people who approach the Church to celebrate a baptism, wedding, or funeral. This is a good thing. They should be welcomed, supported, and encouraged. But it can be hard going, because while the parents primarily want to announce their newborn to the world, the husband and wife want to celebrate their love for each other, and the family wants to celebrate the life of the one they mourn, the Church is focused on celebrating Christ. It is

Christ who initiates and saves all the baptized. It is Christ whose sacrificial love for us finds a deep expression in married love. It is the mercy and love of Christ who receives our dead. You can start to see the pastoral tension. While it should never be an either/or, we have all been to some sacraments where Christ was lucky to get a mention amidst the celebration of the individuals involved. Take eulogies, for example. The longest one I have ever sat through went for one hour and six minutes. And some say priests are long-winded! I knew we were in trouble when after forty minutes the eulogist said, "Then in 1963..." We still had a long way to go. The tension in liturgy today is that this celebration is not about an abstraction, it is Christ present and active in the lives of real people in real time. Both matter.

Knowing that God meets us in our need, even at liturgy, comes from experience. I was ordained a priest at the Jesuit parish of North Sydney in 1993. I was ordained on December 11, 1993, with a good friend Michael McGirr. I was supposed to be ordained at Brisbane, the capital of my home state, but for a whole variety of Jesuit reasons, I was asked to join Michael in Sydney. Despite being friends, I can remember being very anxious as I rang him with this suggestion, imagining that he may prefer to be ordained on his own, in his home parish, where his family had been pillars of the parish for generations. After a pause in the conversation, which I mistakenly took to be displeasure, he said, "Well, Dickie" (Michael is one of the few people who get away with calling me that) "this is a huge relief. You're more interested in liturgy than I am, so why don't we agree that you organize the ceremony and I'll just turn up." It didn't quite work out like that, but it did move in that direction.

Christopher Willcock, SJ, our Australian Jesuit composer, and I called in a few musician friends to help out. We put together a seventy-voice choir, the brass and timpani from the Sydney Symphony Orchestra, and soloists from Opera Australia. As you can tell, it was a very simple, low-key event!

In planning that ordination, I missed two things. The first was that that summer's night would be one of the hottest and most humid days anyone could remember. The temperature got to 102 degrees (38 Celsius). When the ceremony commenced at 8:00 p.m. it was still 82 (27 Celsius). The second thing was that on that very night, directly across the road from the church on the North Sydney Oval, the Salvation Army was conducting "Carols by Candlelight." It started at 8:00 p.m. as well. As the procession snaked its way to the back of the church and up the stairs, all we could hear from the loud speakers booming across the road was "I'm Dreaming of a White Christmas." I know that I was so hot, I was too!

Michael and I had eight hundred of our closest family and friends packed into this church with no air conditioning. The competition from the Salvos, however, meant that the people at the back couldn't hear very well. Rather than anything of the ceremony, all they could hear was "Jingle bells, jingle bells, jingle all the way." So what did they do? They closed the windows and doors. Watching this happen from the sanctuary was one thing, but then we felt a wave of heat roll up the church. More than a little nervous and under the lights and the vestments, the sanctuary had become a sauna.

During the singing of Father Willcock's splendid Trocaire Gloria, I thought to myself, "I'm not feeling very well," and sat down. Then I thought, "I'm *really* not feeling very well," and went to put my head between my legs—not quite the pose I wanted to strike at my ordination. And as I did, I passed out on the floor.

Now, videos are wonderful things! Mine shows that as I sat down, my mother got out of the front pew, walked up on the sanctuary, and was there in time to catch me as I fell. I fell into my mother's arms. I have always thought that Sigmund Freud would have had a field day with this moment—widowed mother catches celibate priest son at his ordination: Oedipus, eat your heart out! My mother loves that part of the video, because not only does it capture her doing what she calls her "Pieta trick," but, because, as she explains, "That was the most expensive dress I have ever purchased in my life, and look, it fell beautifully on the floor. That dress was worth every cent I paid for it!"

I discovered that night that nothing stops a Father Christopher Willcock *Gloria*. When I asked him later what he would've done if I had died, he laughed and said, "I would have said, 'Ladies and gentlemen of the choir and the band, please turn to the Requiem Mass at the back.'"

Once the *Gloria* had concluded, the bishop—who was, for good measure, presiding at his first ordination ever—asked if there was a doctor in the congregation. This was a Jesuit ordination, so soon I was surrounded by a team of twelve doctors and a couple of nurses. I could have had every part of my anatomy dealt with by a specialist. It was just a heavy faint, but when I came to, the bishop wondered out loud what to do next. My then provincial, Fr. William Uren, SJ, told the bishop, "Well, we're not coming back tomorrow." And with that, Michael was dispatched to take me to the sacristy to have a walk around and a drink and to return when I was ready. When we got to the sacristy, I plaintively said to Michael, "I'm so sorry, Mick, I've ruined our ordination." "Don't be sorry, Dickie," he replied, "I'm not nervous at all now, because I can't do anything more to muck this liturgy up than what you've already done."

Meanwhile, what was happening in the church was a study in human nature. Because my father died of a stroke at the age of thirty-six, I knew my immediate and extended family would be anxious that a serious episode had occurred. On the other side of the aisle, the McGirrs were understandably saying, "That Richard Leonard is such a show-off! It was our Michael's night and now the focus is all on him." Across the aisle, my side was filling in the McGirr side about our family's medical history—so much so that, when Michael and I emerged from the sacristy, you would swear Lazarus had just come out of the tomb. After the mandatory canonical questions were asked and before we proceeded on, I knew for my family's sake it was important that I speak so that they could be relieved that I had not suffered a stroke. The bishop agreed. I told the congregation, "You've just seen a perfectly planned liturgy go completely down the gurgler. So we better just get on with it." And the crowd burst into supportive applause all over again.

Later that night, a Jesuit theologian told me, "This was the best ordination I have ever attended." I was curious given that the style of music and liturgy that night would not have been to his taste. He tends to be a Kumbaya-my-Lord-on-a-bad-guitar kinda guy. "I don't know if you noticed," I replied, "but I passed out during the Gloria." "Yes, that's what made it really great." "Why's that?" "Well," he continued excitedly, "as we were coming in the procession singing Chris's glorious arrangement of 'All Creatures of Our God and King,' you could not help but be filled with how great God is. And then, within a short time, you collapsed on the floor. It acted out the central drama of every liturgy: that God is great and we are frail, that God looks on us in our frailty and sent Christ to sustain and support us in and through the Church. We come to public prayer because in our frailty we need God's grace to help us witness to the gospel. That's what made this the best ordination I have ever attended."

God is great and we are frail and we need Christ's grace in and through the Church to help us witness to the gospel.

The seven sacraments are unique moments where we believe God comes to us in special ways. Baptism, Eucharist, penance, confirmation, marriage, holy orders, and the anointing of the sick are, as St. Augustine says, "an outward and visible sign of an inward and invisible grace." When we come to pray publicly what links the sacraments? Apart from what was said earlier, they all require the word of God to be read; they all have a rhythm and flow, action and contemplation; they all involve touch and engage the senses; and they all mark a rite of passage.

THE WORD OF GOD

Dan Brown did Christianity a favor in writing *The Da Vinci Code*. What this book, and later the film, did was to expose the level of ignorance among Christians about their own history and how the New Testament was compiled. It is much to our shame that Mr. Brown has been the first person to tell a host of biblically illiterate Catholics, and other Christians besides, that the New Testament was not a first-century version of the Book of Mormon, falling from the sky. It's not Dan Brown's fault that the religious education of most of us was so poor that we were never told that the revelation of our sacred texts came through a prolonged and passionate fight over the centuries about what was in and out. Hebrews, James, Revelation, and 1 and 2 Peter, and not the four canonical Gospels, were the highly disputed texts. It was not until 633 that the Council of Toledo finally decreed that the fights were over and that the twenty-seven books we now call the New Testament were accepted.

And it is not even the fault of most Catholics that we didn't know this, because we were warned off reading the Bible; the study of its history or compilation was a Protestant concern at best, or a sin against accepting it as Holy Writ. One of the best gifts of the Second Vatican Council has been the promotion of the Sacred Scriptures for private prayer and study.

Given that some prayer is better than no prayer is one of the dictums of my life, wherever possible it should include some sort of meditation on the word of God, especially on the gospel.

GATHERING WITH THE ASSEMBLY

In an increasingly hostile world to religion, having and holding faith can be a very arduous business. We need each other and are not meant to be soldiering on our own. There was a good reason Jesus left behind a community. Christ was never under any illusions about the cost of following his lead, but he underlined how much we need each other to survive in this world. And we need his protection. We often like to feel so self-sufficient these days that we bristle when we hear how Christ "protects" us, but that is precisely what he does. And that protection comes through prayer, reading the word, celebrating the sacraments, and participating in the life of the Church. Unfortunately, local Catholic assemblies can leave a little to be desired. It would be very foolish to note falling rates of practicing Catholics in every Western country of which I am aware, and blame it all on secularism. That plays its role for sure, but it has been my constant experience that good liturgy enlivens faith and bad liturgy deadens it.

A few years back, there was a survey done across several English-speaking countries. They asked Catholics eighteen to thirty-five (the fastest disappearing group in the Church) the following: What keeps you coming to Sunday Mass? The overwhelming top three responses were (1) a warm and hospitable community, (2) good music and good preaching, and (3) a community that practices what it preaches.

WARMTH AND HOSPITALITY

One of the big issues in liturgy in the Catholic Church concerns who is welcome and who is not. Let's get really clear, the official teaching of the Church remains that only those who are in "a state of grace" can receive holy communion. The way some people speak about who they think are in or not in a state of grace and therefore should or should not be receiving holy communion leads me to conclude that they work out of a "shape up or ship out" model of membership. The problem with this position is that it is irreconcilable with the practice of Jesus.

We are welcoming and hospitable to others in God's name because God is extravagantly hospitable to us. While every group has its boundaries and there are limits to what people can dissent from, we could take the earliest Church as our model and stay open to our doubters for as long as we possibly can and so help them realize the transforming truth that has changed our lives.

GOOD MUSIC AND GOOD PREACHING

Bishops, priests, and deacons spend a good deal of time preparing and giving homilies. Unfortunately, this does not necessarily make them good. A cursory glance at our seminary syllabus reveals that, in nearly every case, we pay less attention to the art and craft of preaching and homiletics than any other Christian denomination. The old days are over when thinking that a solid theological and biblical education was sufficient. These days the competition for the minds, hearts, and souls of our young people is as fierce as ever.

One question is whether we give our preachers feedback about what they communicate—knowing that what is said and what is being communicated can be two very different things. Sometimes a pastor is so loved and respected that he gets away with a mediocre homily, because the best homily he gives is the way he lives. While others might give great homilies, their lives do not reflect the simplicity, humility, and charity that are a hallmark of our Christians leaders.

When we come to preach, one size does not fit all, but from surveys of Catholics, we know there are four consistent gripes about homilies that detract from public prayer being prayerful: they are too long; the congregation cannot understand the accent of the homilist; they are over the heads of the congregation; and they do not intersect with the assembly's daily lives.

Music should follow similar lines. There is such a variation between parishes, dioceses, and countries in the way music is selected and performed. Sadly, these days it is often a question of how wealthy a parish is as to how accomplished their music program may be. A general rule in the English-speaking world is that the United States leads the field in the overall professionalism of its music ministry, not only because the donations are also higher but because, rightly in my opinion, the money claimed on the parish budget for music and liturgy is considered under the category of "the greatest good for the greatest number."

We need to be careful of a few things. While our music and liturgy should be done with beauty and grace, we need to avoid turning our worship into a show. The liturgy, by definition, is a sacred drama. While it contains inherent dramatic qualities, our prayer is better served when we are engaged, rather than entertained. Unfortunately, in the name of entertainment and the limitations of some musicians, only one style or genre of music is presented and sung. Older hymns and music from our rich Catholic Tradition, however, can be great vehicles of prayer. I am as worried about someone who will not sing something because "it's old hat" as much as someone who thinks anything written after 1900 is suspect. A wide repertoire aids the greatest number for the greatest good.

The criteria for selecting good music are the following: complementing what each part of the liturgy intends to achieve, supporting the assembly's prayer, and meeting the right need. Some liturgies and music should tap the emotional aspects of our faith more than they do. We should have no trouble in touching the heart, but we need to avoid emotionalism, where the congregation is meant to cry on cue. Allied to this is avoiding gimmicks. The Church's liturgy, when done in the way Vatican II envisaged, is powerful and beautiful. Public prayer is formal and stylized. But that does not mean it has to be alienating and remote.

BEARING WITNESS

If the goal of our full, conscious, and active participation in liturgical prayer is, as the Church says, to send us out to witness to Christ in the world, then let us examine our language. We use a whole range of words to describe what the earliest Christians simply called the breaking of the bread (Acts 2:46). *Eucharist* comes from a Greek word meaning "to give thanks." *Liturgy* is Greek too, meaning "a ritual." *Mass* is from the Latin word *missa*, meaning "to be sent." So when we say we are going to Mass, we are saying we are going to our commissioning to live out the gospel in our daily or weekly lives. Therefore, every liturgy should have some element of how we are to live God's justice in the world.

Public prayer matters because I am saved not just as an individual; we are saved as the people of God. We need each other to rise to that invitation as we come together to pray in an assembly that stands before mystery, in awe and wonder, is hospitable, expresses ancient faith, and works for justice right here and now. While we always celebrate what Christ is doing in sacraments, it is also Christ who is not just in heaven but who meets us in the everyday and normal experiences of our lives. God's greatness meets our frailty. Now that's something to shout and sing about.

25.

MARY AND THE SAINTS

At its best, our prayer with, and devotion to, Mary and the saints should be human, responsive, and adaptable. And it can be now. When we understand the history, dynamism, and depth of our tradition about Mary, we appreciate how it comes out of real communities who were asking real questions of their faith. Some of these may not be as alive or applicable today, but the way we pray with Mary does not have to drip in piety. There is nothing sentimental and pious about the Magnificat in Luke's Gospel. In this great hymn, Mary proclaims that God, through Jesus, will show strength by scattering people's pride, tearing down the mighty from their thrones, and raising up the poor in their place. God will fill the hungry and send away empty the rich, who have not shared. In this, the promise of salvation will be fulfilled for *all* people.

The best place from which to start a contemporary approach to Mary is to heed the advice of Paul VI in his great Marian document, *Marialis Cultus*, and begin with the ten episodes about Mary in the New Testament:

Mary knew what it is like to be a pregnant thirteen-year-old girl with an eighteen-year-old fiancé who was not the father of the child. Imagine the potential shame. On a human level, the visitation is the meeting of two cousins—both unexpectedly pregnant in the most extraordinary circumstances—in the mountains (the hill country) where God has always been manifest to the Israelites. Elizabeth embodies the Old Covenant while Mary embodies the

New, and final, Covenant in Jesus. In the nativity, Jesus is born to homeless, poor parents one hundred miles (160 km) from Nazareth. The presentation of the Child Jesus in the temple tells us the Holy Family were devout Jews. The flight into Egypt may be a theological story about Jesus being the new Moses, but it is also the Church's defense of the poor refugees against tyrants.

Later, it takes Joseph and Mary two days to know he is gone, and when they find him, they do not understand why he had done this to them. I know a few mothers and fathers who can empathize with them. In Mark 3, Mary goes to bring Jesus home from his public ministry, which gives consolation to a parent who cannot really work out his or her children, what path they are taking, and where it will end. At Cana, Mary saves the bride and groom from shame by having Jesus perform the first sign of John's Gospel, one about endless joy (wine), where heaven and earth are wed (the banquet) and shame is no more. Every Gospel tells us that Mary knew what it was like to stand there and watch her only child capitally punished. Mary has something to say to any parent who has ever lost a child in death, before or after they were born. Finally, at Pentecost, Mary is in the center of the earliest Church as it begins its mission in Christ's name to set people free, to reap a new harvest, and to declare that humanity is debt free.

Even these few reflections on Mary's role in the life of Jesus enable us to let go of a plaster statue and be accompanied by a flesh and blood woman, mother, sister, saint, prophet, and friend. To reclaim our prayer to and with her, it is good to be reminded that she was fully and truly human. Mary is not God. She needed God's redemption in Christ and this poor, simple Jewish woman is the preeminent disciple of the kingdom Jesus proclaimed.

The religious truths contained in the Scriptures cannot lead us astray in our spiritual lives, and these texts provide enough flesh and blood moments for our prayer that can intersect with our real lives. They also serve as the ways in which Mary can bring us together ecumenically.

As an enjoyable aside, let me tell you about the best nativity play I have ever seen. In 1994, I was invited by an elderly nun to be the guest of honor at the Sacred Heart Primary School's nativity play in Melbourne. The school is a great mix of children from the wealthier inner city terrace houses and from the high-rise housing projects. That year, it was the turn of grade three (eight years of age) to perform the play.

When I arrived, Sister told me that she had trouble with the boy who was playing the innkeeper because he had his heart set on playing St. Joseph. "He is a Muslim boy and I really thought I should at least have a Christian, if not a Catholic boy playing St. Joseph." Rehearsals had not gone well, but she was sure everything would be fine in the performance.

The whole school was there along with all the parents of grade three. In the front row of the school hall was the principal, Sister, and me.

As Mary and Joseph knocked on the makeshift wall that was the inn's door, the innkeeper gruffly yelled out, "Who's there?" "I am Joseph and this is my wife, Mary, and we have nowhere to stay tonight and she is having a baby." (Having a baby? If her baby bump was anything to go by, that girl was having octuplets!) The innkeeper did not budge. Sister leaned forward and said in a loud stage whisper, "Ahmed, you know what to do, darling. You know your lines. Open the door and make your very important speech." He didn't budge.

So Sister told Joseph to knock again. The innkeeper barked more angrily, "Who's there?" We got Joseph's speech again, but the little innkeeper didn't move. The tension was rising in that room now, so Sister leaned forward again and in a stronger voice said, "Ahmed, your Mom and Dad are here, darling, and they will be so proud of you. Now just play your part and make us all proud." Sister then told Joseph to knock for the third time, and he gave out his speech again. Now, before Ahmed could decide what to do next, a loud bass African voice came from the back of the room, "Ahmed, you open that goddamn door or I'll belt your bum!" I turned around to see the largest human being I have ever seen. Ahmed's father, Mohammed, was a refugee to Australia from Sierra Leone. He was six feet eight inches tall and told me he weighed in at 238 lbs (17 stone) of solid body mass. So proud was he that his son had a starring role in the Christmas play that he was dressed in his magnificent white celebratory kaftan with a small white cap on his head. Now, however, he was coming down the aisle toward the stage, and every adult there was thinking, "Open the door, open the door, open the goddamn door, because I think your bum belted by this guy is going to hurt." Someone intercepted Mohammed as Ahmed opened the door and said plaintively to Mary, "You can come in," but then shouted at Joseph, "but Joseph you can piss off!" With that, Joseph burst into tears, the shepherds and the three wise men started a fight with the innkeeper "because he said a rude word," and Sister stood up, turned to everyone and said, "This wasn't the way it was supposed to go." It took ten minutes to restore peace.

It was the best nativity play I have ever seen. God is good with mess.

RECLAIMING MARY NOW

For thousands of years, Mary, first among the saints, and all the saints who have followed her, have given us models of faith, companions on the journey of prayer, and support in our prayer. These days Mary is either given too much attention (for some she can even seem to displace the Holy Spirit) or she is given next to no attention at all. It is also scandalous that except for the Orthodox, High Church Anglicans, and the Catholics, Mary has been a dividing line between the churches over the years. We can now reclaim this long and extraordinary tradition in a way that is sane, ecumenical, inclusive, liberating, and catholic. It is worth bothering about.

It's amazing to think that only until a few years ago, at home, at school, and in the parish and diocese, we had so many devotions to Mary and then, seemingly and mysteriously, they vanished overnight. I can remember: Novena to the Blessed Virgin Mary; the Children of Mary; the family rosary; the rosary statue; May and October altars; scapulas; medals; sodalities; the Legion of Mary; the Teams of Our Lady; the numerous congregations of sisters, brothers, and priests named in honor of Our Lady; how many sisters had "Mary" in their religious names; how some parishes had processions on various Marian feast days; and Catholic kids used to get holidays on the Feasts of the Assumption and the Immaculate Conception—that was among the best things in attending Catholic school.

My most affectionate and early memory of devotion to Mary was the rosary. From the time I was eight, I spent most of my holidays at my Uncle Maurice and Aunty Claire's ranch in the outback of Australia. I come from a large extended Irish/Australian Catholic family. Maurice Leonard was the patriarch of the nine Leonard children. He used to call each family before the school holidays and invite his nieces and nephews for the vacation. There could be up to ten cousins on holiday there at any one time. It's only now I think of Aunty Claire having to cook, clean, and wash for that crowd.

Uncle Maurice and Aunty Claire were married in 1948. Every day until Uncle Maurice died a few years ago, they said the rosary. And even though the nightly devotion was falling off in our homes as children in the 1970s, when we went to their ranch for holidays, we would all kneel after dinner and recite the five decades. Because Maurice and Claire had become so used to each other's patterns of prayer, they had a very distinctive way of "giving out" the Hail Mary and responding with the Holy Mary. Uncle Maurice would say, "Hail Mare mingum, blest la jim." By the time Maurice got to "mingum," which I assume was "among women," Claire would start "Whole may may mem." And so it went: "Hail Mare mingum, blest la jim/Whole may may mem" They were speaking in tongues long before it was trendy! If any of the cousins were too slow in actually saying "Hail Mary, full of grace...," Uncle Maurice would say, "Speed it up, Rich." So, if you can't beat 'em, join 'em, and so we all said, "Hail Mare mingum, blest la jim. Whole may may mem." Of course, Claire and Maurice rightly understood that the rosary was a mantra prayer. We are not meant to meditate on every word of every prayer but to use the words to still our minds and focus on the chapter of Jesus' life in each mystery. This is precisely what they did.

The other features of Uncle Maurice's rosary were what he called the "toppings and tailings." These were all the prayers before and after the rosary, do you remember them? They felt like they went longer than the rosary did. We said the Apostles' Creed, the Benedictus, and the Magnificat before, and then prayers to the Sacred Heart, for the conversion of Russia (that worked!), and for the protection of the pope (that worked too!).

About eighteen years on from when I started holidaying on the family ranch, I decided to enter the Jesuits. One of my other cousins, who went to that ranch as often as I did, took me out for dinner. Given what I was doing with my life, matters religious were on the agenda. Out of nowhere my cousin said across the table "Hail Mare mingum, blest la jim" to which I immediately replied, "Whole may may mem." And back and forth it went for a while until the waiter asked us which Eastern Bloc country we came from! During the meal, we recalled lots of happy memories of those summer holidays, including saying the rosary. At one stage, my cousin said, "There was one weird prayer Uncle Maurice used to say in the tailings, do you remember it, when he hit his chest?" "What was weird about it?" I asked. "Well, it's a bit strange, don't you think, to hit your chest and call out, 'Say G'day to Jesus' and then everyone replies, 'Have Mercy on us.'" Now, this is an Australian moment, but my uncle had a very broad Australian accent. What my cousin thought was "Say G'day to Jesus" was in fact "Sacred Heart of Jesus." And at that moment, I could hear my uncle saying it, and could well understand how a young boy thought his uncle was "Saying G'day to Jesus," to which we all called back, "Have mercy on us." This was a tough religion!

We have lost something important as we quickly moved away from those family practices. But it is more than possible to have a very healthy devotion to Mary as first among the saints, as a companion to us in the journey of faith, as a prophet and as a mother.

MOTHER OF THE POOR

My own devotion to Mary re-entered my adult life. First, however, I need to tell you that when I was in grade four of my Catholic School, Sr. Mary Wenceslaus, RSM, was our music teacher. She came into class one day and taught us the twelfth-century Latin prayer to Our Lady, Salve Regina. Hold that thought.

On the August 15, 1975, eight members of a village in the mountain country well above the capital of Chile were arrested by the military police. They were accused of being terrorists and organizing labor unions. They were innocent of the former and proudly guilty of the latter. For months, the villagers tried to find out where the men had gone and why they had been taken away.

As we now know, abduction, torture, and illegal imprisonment were daily realities for Chilean people under General Pinochet.

Word arrived in November that the corpses of the parish councillors could be found in Santiago's morgue. My friend, Sr. Catherine, was an Australian nun working in that parish. She took the mothers of the eight men to the morgue in Santiago. Catherine later wrote to me, "Richard, you could not imagine what we found in the morgue. There were over a hundred corpses piled high on each other, and our mothers had to roll someone else's son over in an attempt to find her own. And as the mothers searched, they began to weep loudly, realizing how evil we can be toward one another. As they wept, they prayed the rosary. As one mother, and then another, found her son, they called out more desperately, 'Holy Mary, Mother of God pray for us sinners now, and at the hour of our death.'"

Catherine's letter continued, "For years I rejected devotion to Mary because I felt oppressed by the way generations of men in the Church presented her—blue veils, white skin, always smiling, a perpetual virgin and yet also a mother, an ideal I could never achieve, but one to which I was told I should aspire. In the experience of the village mothers, however, the distortions of who Mary was for a poor and suffering world faded away. Far from feeling distant from their devotion, I found myself praying with them, knowing that Mary was with us in our shock, anger, and grief."

The letter went on, "What happened next was indescribable. Twenty soldiers stood by and watched nine women load eight corpses into my truck. They never lifted a finger to help us. We could only get seven out of the eight in the back, so one of the mothers cradled her son in her arms in the front with me. The journey took four hours. On the long trip home, we prayed the rosary again and again. As the mother next to me said at one stage, 'We pray with Mary at times like this because she knows what it's like to bring a child into the world and claim his dead body in her arms.' And there it was, right beside me for the four-hour trip into the mountains. Something changed in me for the better that day."

Twelve years later, in 1989, Catherine died of hepatitis in that village. Her family had been trying to get her to come home for months, but she lied about how ill she was and said that she had everything she needed there. The only consolation Catherine's family got was when a letter arrived from the mothers in the village. When I had it translated from Spanish into English it read,

> We want you to know that we were with Catherine when she died. We would never have let her die alone for she was one of our children too. We often prayed the rosary with her. She seemed to like that, thumbing the beads she used ever since she brought us back with our boys. We have buried her next to our sons and put on her tombstone the line she asked us to inscribe, "Mary my friend, my companion and mother of the poor, pray for me."

In 2010, I was the first member of both Catherine's family and friends to go to Chile. I caught a bus from Santiago, and nearly five hours later alighted at 2:00 p.m. The five surviving mothers were waiting for me. They took me immediately to the cemetery, and there I found Catherine's grave among the eight men who were killed in 1975. There was the inscription on her grave in English and Spanish. We all stood and wept. Then one of the women asked me to pray. They had very little English. All I could say in Spanish was *lo siento, no hablo español*. But then, like a good steward who brings out of the storehouse both things new and old, I remembered Sr. Mary Wenceslaus. (See facing page.) By the end of that ancient love song, we were all singing and crying and hugging.

When I am in the shadow of death and the valley of tears, I turn to Mary and the saints because I need all the help I can get. Now is not the time to throw out devotion to Mary, but to reclaim a relationship with her as prophet, friend, and companion in faith. If we are in touch with the facts of her life and how we came to have what we have now in our tradition, and are poor enough in spirit, then that's where the mother of the poor meets us and gently leads us to her Son.

S Álve, Regína,* máter mi-se-ricórdi-ae : Ví-ta, dulcé-

do, et spes nóstra, sálve. Ad te clamámus, éxsu-les, fí-

li- i Hévae. Ad te suspi-rámus, geméntes et fléntes in hac

lacrimárum válle. E-ia ergo, Advocáta nóstra, íllos tú-os

mi-se-ricórdes ócu-los ad nos convérte. Et Jésum, benedí-

ctum frúctum véntris tú- i, nóbis post hoc exsí-li-um ostén-

de. O clémens : O pí- a : O dúlcis * Vírgo Ma-rí- a.

26.

THE EFFECTS OF PRAYER

As noted earlier, over recent centuries often the reason we prayed was to "save our soul" or to "get to heaven." Although we might couch this reason in different terms today, it has not changed, but we have added to it, and rightly so. While the Gospels are clear about attaining heaven, they are equally strong about bringing heaven to bear on this world right here and now. Both aspects are needed. Prayer that is overly focused on otherworldly concerns is not in touch with daily life. It can quickly become formalism. Prayer that has too much emphasis on this world without an eye on the next can become a political campaign with no sense that, even if we fall short of establishing the reign of God here, then the full realization of Christ's kingdom still awaits us.

So the reason Christians seek to encounter the presence of God and maintain an intimate and loving relationship with him is because we are on a mission: Christ's mission. In what is called the Great Commission, Jesus sends out his disciples to continue the world he established. "All authority in heaven and on earth has been given to me. Go therefore and make disciples of all nations, baptizing them in the name of the Father and of the Son and of the Holy Spirit, and teaching them to obey everything that I have commanded you. And remember, I am with you always, to the end of the age" (Matt 28:18–20).

Note well what Jesus did not say. He did not say to wait at

home until the world comes to you, talking your talk and walking your walk. In Western societies, we have become very used to the world coming to us on our (the Church's) terms. It is understandable. The numbers were so large for so long that our most urgent sense of being on mission with Christ was gaining converts so we could assure them of getting to heaven. I knew a Jesuit priest who used to ask everyone he met, "Are you a Catholic?" and if the response was in the negative, he would quickly follow it up with, "but I am sure you would like to be." It did the trick in starting countless spiritual conversations. As good a mission as it remains to invite people into the life of the Church, it is clear from the way Jesus lived that he also had a broader agenda for us and his mission as well.

A SINFUL CHURCH

These days, one of the greatest obstacles to people coming to praise, reverence, and serve God in the Church is the Church itself. Because the Lord sends us out to the real world, not the world we would prefer to evangelize, we need to listen very carefully to the fact that, currently, in the religious censuses or surveys in every Western democracy, the fastest growing groups either do not believe in God or do not want to belong to any religion or church. Churches are on the nose.

Another interesting group is that of the fellow travelers whom I call "cultural Catholics." These people freely and knowingly say they are Catholic, but do not participate in any way in the life of the Church. Maybe they come for Christmas. In the United States, they might race into the church for ashes on the first day of Lent. But they are not there at Easter—those numbers are falling—and less frequently for baptism, marriages, and funerals (hatching, matching, and dispatching as it's sometimes called). In Western countries, those ceremonies are decreasing, while civil naming, marrying, and burying rites have risen exponentially in the last twenty years. In these instances, belonging to the Church is tribal, a cultural definition in a similar way to some branches of Judaism where someone will proudly say they are Jewish, but they do not keep a kosher kitchen or observe the dietary laws, rarely keep the Sabbath, sparingly attend the Synagogue, and do not mark the high holy days. So there is a precedent for what might be emerging in Western Catholicism.

WITNESS IN WORD AND ACTION

Christian witness has two component parts, one much more important than the other: what we say and what we do. For all the complexities of philosophy and theology, the Christian message is a relatively simple one: to be a follower of Jesus we have to love God, love our neighbor, and love ourselves. I am sometimes amused by some Catholic parents who are angry because their children attend CCD or a Catholic school and say, "But they don't know the Ten Commandments." I am all for them knowing the Ten Commandments, that famous summary of the hundreds of Mosaic laws given by God to the chosen people, but it is Jesus himself who says that all religious law can be fulfilled if we love God, neighbor, and self. Love of self has had a mixed history in the Christian story, but it is essential for prayer and mission, and not just because Jesus said it. Self-love is often confused with self-adoration. Nothing could be further from what Jesus is saying. If we have no sense of our own self-worth, our own dignity, and the personal love God has for each of us, it is impossible for us to give the same to others and to claim from others the dignity we deserve. We will either treat others as our inferiors on the one hand, or allow others to walk all over us on the other. Love of self is not about canonizing a loss of self-control. Jesus shows us by the way he loved his Father, us, and himself that true love always involves sacrifice. If we love our self in the right way, we have the self-control to forego those things that are most destructive in our lives, and we have the generosity to do for others the things that will enrich their lives. Jesus knew that we can never love others if we hate ourselves.

If we are witnessing by the words we use, it is essential to get the basic message right because words define reality.

All that most people hear about Church, religion, and faith in the public square each day is bad news because we do not communicate these facts to our own and the wider community. It is not a question of canceling out the crimes and shame of what has happened in recent years; rather, the good Spirit helps us see that the bad news story is not the only story and that, as weak and sinful as we are, our witness by action is already there, every day, in season and out of season. We need to bring it into the light, not to glorify ourselves, but to "boast in the Lord," to highlight that this is what Christ the teacher, the healer, the one who raises up the poor, and the Good Shepherd achieves in and through us.

The best prayer is always rooted in reality, and so knowing the facts as we go out with Christ to the world is pivotal to what our prayer on mission is about. There are many good news stories too.

ENCULTURATION

When our prayer sends us out to witness by word and deed, we better know who we are, who we are going to, and where we will be witnessing. These are tasks of an enculturated faith. An enculturated faith is centered on Jesus. While this is so obvious, it is also very critical. If we have no loving relationship with Jesus, then we have no reason to be on his mission, no frame of personal experience through which we can process our membership of the Church. But Jesus is rarely the problem. Most people like Jesus, they like what he says, and they like what he did. The Church can be the deal breaker.

If the Church is on mission, then enculturation demands that we know to whom we are sent. We have to confront our national and world culture as it is, not as we would like it to be. We cannot be on mission to a culture we do not know or to one that we simply despise. Jesus himself lived in a kingdom that was a client-state of a brutal imperial power. Palestine was, on the whole, a desperately poor country. There were also significant religious divisions, whose leaders were hostile to Jesus' message. Yet as nearly every page of the Gospels tells us, Jesus knew his audience, and so should we. Why is it, for example, that at every evangelization conference I have ever attended, we begin by talking about the

Church, ourselves, when we should start by talking about the world and the people to whom we are sent to proclaim the gospel?

This is the issue for our prayer and action if we are going out to this world: If Christ does not send most of us to any other country than the one into which we were born, then what do we have to say to a population that is aging, where most people are not in traditional family structures, have small families, are completely urbanized and mobile, are affluent by world standards but spend a quarter of their incomes on their mortgage, are still generally monocultural, like to gamble, drink, suffer from depression, love sports and pornography, are well educated by world standards but do not read heavy books or magazines, and only go near a church for weddings, baptisms, and funerals?

LIBERATION

Complementing our witness in word and deed and our enculturated faith that attends to the real world with realistic expectations of what we can do for those to whom we are sent, the Church says that our mission should be about liberation—setting people free so that they might have the freedom of the sons and daughters of God.

When we hear the word *liberation*, we might sometimes think of liberation theology, where the demands of the gospel call us to actual social and political action to make the world a more just place. The liberation we seek could be that in some circumstances, but more likely it will be to continue what the Church is already doing well, offering the very best education, healthcare, welfare, and pastoral care possible. For centuries, these have been effective instruments of opting for the poor and the marginalized, and of humanizing and conscientizing the wealthy and the powerful—all areas where our efforts need to be increased.

We can increase our efforts, first, by being as compassionate toward others as Jesus is toward us. That doesn't mean abandoning our principles and beliefs. It means that in judging the world, we should pray to see it as God sees it. Sometimes, unfortunately, it is not what some men and women in the Church say in the public square, it is how they say it, the attitude they bring to bear, and how they can appear to condemn anyone who disagrees with them.

Compassion also asks everyone in the Church to imagine in prayer what it's like to be a person of color, a refugee, a victim of domestic violence, gay, lesbian, or transgendered, divorced and remarried, or disabled. In our mission to set others free, whenever we catch ourselves jumping to an immediate condemnation of someone, let's stop and pray that our first response might be, "What must life be like for you?" At that point, our mission to them will be touching on the divine.

Second, we need to liberate people from some frightening theology about where the God of love fits into a world of pain and suffering. We believe that God made woman and man as a self-expression of divine and undeserved love. God made the universe and everything in it not out of divine need but out of desire for our happiness. We are meant to grow and develop and have our being in God's creation. To safeguard against us feeling like pawns, God enabled the gifts of consciousness and free will to evolve so that we can make choices—even the possibility of our choosing against God.

Third, our prayer and mission should be marked by joy. My friend and Jesuit brother, James Martin, SJ, has explored how central this theme is in the Christian life in his book *Between Heaven and Mirth*. Personally, I have lost count of how many parents and grandparents say to me, "Father, my children (or grandchildren) do not practice their faith. What am I going to do?" I always reply, "The most important thing you can do has nothing to do with what you should say, but the joy with which you live your life. You may not be around to see it, but I have been at wakes where unchurched family members lament that they are lacking the joy that their mother or father found in their faith. That can be the beginning of something wonderful."

There are real challenges, too, in the way priests welcome people at Mass, and at baptisms, weddings, and funerals. I am appalled every time I hear how a priest began a packed Christmas Mass by berating members of the congregation for actually turning up, saying, "Why aren't you here every week?" Why would they return? Why not thank them for coming, welcome them home for Christmas, and at the end invite them to come back any week, every week.

Furthermore, before we spend even more money on expensive programs of evangelization, let's start with the moments where the Church touches the most people every week: at baptisms, weddings, and funerals. If we did these as well as we possibly can, I am sure that our witness to Christ through his sacraments would bear fruit. To that end, during my opening remarks on these ritual occasions, I always say, "Long gone are the days, thank God, when anyone who is not a Catholic should feel anything but very welcome in this Church today. Whether you are of another Christian denomination, another faith tradition (a Jew, Muslim, Buddhist, or Hindu), or even if you don't share our belief in God, you are very welcome here today, and I hope you will join in all the parts of the ceremony you feel you can." This costs me nothing, extends the sort of inclusive hospitality for which the Lord was known, and does untold good. It is certainly far better than starting the liturgy by telling everyone who can and cannot receive holy communion. There may be a time to say that very sensitively later in the liturgy, but to begin by saying who is excluded at the Lord's Table is a pastoral disaster.

Fourth, our prayer and mission should be all about gratitude. On nearly every world lifestyle indicator, even if we are doing tough at present, we live in the most privileged of circumstances. As Christians, we do not think this is our right, our due, or our good fortune. As Christians, we know this is a blessing, and we respond to it every day by just being grateful.

Fifth, our mission must be one of preaching and practicing forgiveness. The two biggest sins that Jesus confronts on nearly every page of the Gospels are hypocrisy—those who say one thing and do another, and lack of forgiveness. This part of Jesus' preaching sets him apart from nearly every other religious leader in history. Jesus kept forgiving people, and he told his disciples to do the same. In following Christ and being on mission, we were never promised an easy ride. In our complex world, no one can pretend that forgiveness is easy or that it is a magic wand we wave over deep hurts and harsh words. True forgiveness does not deny reality; it deals with it with justice and compassion. But forgiveness is necessary if we are going to follow Jesus. Revenge and spite, so endemic in society, are the antithesis of what Jesus taught and lived out.

Some of us recall the 1970 hit film *Love Story*, with its outrageous motto: "Love means never having to say you're sorry." Well, this might have been fine for Ali and Ryan, but let's be very clear, such an attitude is irreconcilable with the gospel of Jesus Christ. As Christians, the exact opposite is the case—we look for opportunities to say "I'm sorry" to those we have hurt, and we work toward being the sort of woman or man who can say "I forgive you," without sounding pompous or being sanctimonious about it. I keep meeting people who have not spoken to family members or friends for years. Clearly, it would be best if they could be reconciled with those who have offended them or those they have hurt, but life is complex. The litmus test for a Christian is whether we even want to or whether we care. Forgiveness is as much a movement in our heart—we long for reconciliation if it could ever happen—as much as it may be something that we see realized in this life. So, if we are on mission with Christ, we better be like him and become famous for our ability to forgive.

Finally, we will be judged about whether our life in the world is Christian by how we live the three great virtues of faith, hope, and love. And what would prayer to a loving God that liberates us—even in the face of pain and suffering—look like? Let me tell you about Jenny.

27.

JENNY AND SEBASTIAN

As I mentioned earlier, my first appointment as a deacon and priest was at St. Canice's in King's Cross, Sydney, the city's red-light district. In my time, on average, the rectory received fifty-six callers a day. It was one of the few parish houses where the clergy did not need to leave the house and still go to bed tired. At 4:00 on a Monday morning in Lent, there was an urgent ringing of the front door bell. Halfway down the stairs, I called out more loudly than I had anticipated doing, "Oh, give it a break, I'm coming!" The doorbell ceased ringing.

When I opened the door, I found a hysterical woman slumped on the top step. I found out later she was twenty-eight years of age, though she looked fifty-eight. Life had not been kind to her. When she could catch her breath, she told me she wanted to get into the church. "I need to say a prayer," she cried. She looked as though she could be stoned on drugs, but my intuition told me to go with it. She followed me. I opened up the church and turned on the lights. As I did, the young woman ran all the way down the aisle to the high altar and stood in front of the tabernacle and screamed a primal scream, the likes of which I have never heard. After I calmed her down sufficiently to sit with me on the front pew, she kept repeating the mantra, "Sebastian's dead. Sebastian's dead. Say a prayer for him; pray for me."

I discovered that her name was Jenny and that she went to give her six-month-old son, Sebastian, his feed at 2:00 a.m. "He wasn't breathing properly, so I took him to the hospital." I still wondered if Jenny was in fact on a trip. "Where is Sebastian now?" I asked. "At St. Vincent's," she replied. St Vincent's was our wonderful, local public hospital run by the Sisters of Charity. It did not treat children, only adults. So now I could test my hallucination theory. "Why don't we go back there now?" Jenny looked up, took me by the hand, and said, "I'll go back there with you." We walked to the neighboring suburb, Jenny sobbing gently all the way. On walking into the accident and emergency department at St. V's, and through the large plate glass window, Mary McGuire, the night charge nurse and one of our parishioners, came running out: "Oh Father, thank God you have bought her back." And with that, she ushered us inside. "She arrived here at 2:30 this morning with a blue baby. She said the child wasn't breathing very well. The little boy had been dead for hours. She wanted us to resuscitate the baby, and when we explained we couldn't and why, she became so upset, she jumped up and fled into the night. We don't have a name or an address or a date of birth for the baby or for the mother. We have called the police to see if they can find her. We are fairly sure it is a SIDS death, but the child is now a coroner's case."

In fact, what happened to Jenny is extraordinary. Understandably devastated at the death of her baby son, she started aimlessly wandering the streets of King's Cross, and by 3:30 a.m., she ended up on a park bench with Con, the then most famous homeless man in the red-light district and our leading Catholic parishioner. Con came to everything at the church, but most eagerly anticipated the food that almost always followed. He listened to Jenny's tragic story, and shared his whiskey bottle with her, until at 3:50 a.m., he declared, "I can't help you, but I know people who can." It was a homeless alcoholic man who brought a grieving mother to the rectory door at 4:00 a.m. It was Con who was urgently ringing the front doorbell until he heard me call out. Then he said to Jenny, "I stole a candle stick from this lot last week and hocked it. They don't like me much at present. I'm pissin' off. You're on your own." Hence, I opened the door to find Jenny and no Con.

When I got Jenny back to the rectory, not only did I hear the story of what had happened to her that morning, but I got her backstory too. She was a woman in prostitution who lived with her physically, sexually, and emotionally violent partner, Greg, who was also her pimp. Greg was Sebastian's father. He had ordered a DNA test to make sure. Jenny and Greg were substance abusers and alcoholics.

To say I was pastorally in over my head would be a gross understatement. By 6:30 a.m., I did not have a clue what to do next, but then I recalled that Mary Maguire had said that the staff thought Sebastian was a SIDS death. I don't know why or how I knew that the local SIDS Association had an emergency help line, but I thank God to this day that I did. I found it and called it, and the very reassuring woman at the other end of the phone said they would send out someone as soon as possible.

You never know when one of your best friends is about to walk into your life. At 8:00 a.m., Annie McNamara walked through the rectory door and in doing so she, her wonderful husband Johnny, and their loving family walked into my life. Johnny, a medical doctor, and Annie, a registered nurse, had lost Monica, their second eldest daughter, to SIDS. One of the ways they dealt with their grief at that time was to volunteer with the SIDS Association for other families going through the same tragedy. Seeing Annie and Jenny talk to each other was a lesson in like-to-like counseling. Annie could touch and console Jenny in a way I would never have been capable of doing.

By 11:00 a.m., Jenny told us she did not want to return to Greg. I found her a bed in a church-run women's refuge perfectly named Mana House. Annie and I accompanied Jenny back to her apartment to get necessities for a couple of days. On the top floor of the worst apartment building in one of the worst parts of town, there was Jenny at her front door, followed closely by Annie, and then me on the stairs. As Jenny went to put the key in the door, she turned to Annie and me and said, "I hope Greg hasn't still got the shotgun." "What shotgun would that be?" I inquired. This was the first we had heard of a shotgun. "This morning, Greg accused me of killing Sebastian, so he got the shotgun out to kill me." I have never considered myself much of a martyr, but even I knew that the mother of four (now mother of six) in front of me should not be the person to follow Jenny into Greg's potential shooting range. I was so brave that I hardly recognized myself! I pushed Annie out of the way and followed Jenny into the apartment.

This apartment was one of the most miserable human habitats I have ever seen in my life; actually it is the smell I remember more than anything else. In the corner of this open-plan room was Greg and the shotgun. He was stark naked and spread-eagle on his double bed, dead to the world asleep—drunk, stoned, or both (at least that was what I was hoping for). Now I have seen enough CSI shows to know that I had to "secure the scene," so I went over to the bed, picked up the gun, and carried it to the opposite corner of the room and piled clothes upon it. Greg stirred but didn't wake. Meanwhile, I joined Annie and Jenny on the enclosed balcony of the apartment, which was the nursery. It was a tale of two rooms. One was not fit for dignified human living, the nursery was neat and clean. Everything was labelled. There were little stuffed panda bears and a sweet scent. These rooms told the story of what Jenny loved and the life she hated.

Sebastian's autopsy took six days, and in that time, Annie and I gained Jenny's trust sufficiently for her to tell us her complex story, so much so that she asked me to contact her parents from whom she had been estranged for five years. They were decent, hardworking people in the neighboring state, who, by Jenny's own admission, did nothing to her that might explain how their only child got into drugs, ran away from home, and later got into prostitution. "I can't talk to them, but you tell them what's happened and where I am." Vera and Jack were initially delighted to hear that their daughter was alive and relatively well, but this phone conversation became excruciatingly painful for all of us when I explained that their grandson they never knew they had had died six days ago. The rest of the tragic tale—Jenny's life—could wait. They said they would fly down to be reunited with Jenny as soon as they could.

That same day, the body was released to the undertakers. There were no suspicious circumstances. The cause of death was "most likely SIDS." The next day, Jenny asked Annie and me to take her to the funeral home to see Sebastian for the last time. "I want you to say some prayers with him." It would be my demanding honor to do so. Jack and Vera were flying in that night. The funeral was scheduled for thirty-six hours after they arrived. It was confronting to walk into the viewing room of the funeral parlor and find an open white casket. They had done a wonderful job with Sebastian; he just looked as though he were asleep. Jenny asked me to say some prayers and then asked Annie and me if she could be alone with her baby for the last time. "Of course you can," said Annie with all the empathy and support within her. We went and sat with the receptionist in the foyer. After ten minutes, Annie said, "I'll just go and see if she is okay." From down the corridor to the viewing rooms, I heard Annie screaming. Racing down to the door, I found Jenny on the floor. She had taken Sebastian out of the casket, laid down on the floor, and with her baby in her left arm she had mainlined a syringe of heroin into her neck. She was committing suicide. Annie kept her awake and alert. I raced back to the receptionist. There is sometimes a black humor moment in situations like this, so when I said to her, "You have to call the ambulance. She's dying in that room. She's committing suicide." The receptionist jumped up and yelled, "Oh my God, no one has ever died here before!" No, I thought, they usually come that way. The ambulance was there within minutes. Jenny was given Narcan and she came around. We spent the rest of the day at the hospital, until I talked the doctors into releasing her into my care rather than as an involuntary admission in the psychiatric unit. She had her child's funeral to attend in the morning. Annie had to go home to care for her family.

Vera and Jack rang to say they had arrived and were staying at a Sydney city hotel. Jenny asked me to accompany her to their hotel room and help her explain her situation. On speaking and seeing their daughter for the first time in five years, they had to touch the grief for a grandchild (their only one) they didn't know they had, find out that Jenny was a woman in prostitution, had an addiction to drugs and alcohol, and that day had attempted suicide. How do you start to take any of this on board? Jack and Vera were salt-of-the-earth people who were about to become lights to the world. What did they do with the enormity of devastating news that now confronted them? They focused on the one positive thing they could—they had been reunited with their child. The story of the prodigal son had never been more real to me than when I left Jenny with her parents that night.

Days before, when we were planning Sebastian's funeral service at St. Canice's, Jenny had asked for only three things: that the song "I Will Always Love You" by Whitney Houston be played; that one of his panda bears be placed next to the little white casket; and that "Amazing Grace," the only hymn she remembered from Sunday school, be sung. We had all three. Jack and Vera supported

Jenny as though she had never left their side. Greg sat in the back row, without the shotgun. When the time came for Jenny to follow her baby's casket out of the church, she marched past it with the angriest and most defiant walk I have ever seen in my life. She rejected all offers of human comfort, jumped in the back seat of the funeral car, held the white casket, and yelled at me, "Come on! Let's get this over and done with!" The naked pain of trauma! The cremation was brief and stark.

Sadly for Vera and Jack and also Annie and me, Jenny went back to Greg, to prostitution, and to alcohol and drugs. She was medicating her pain by inflecting more of it on herself. I would sometimes see her around King's Cross and say, "Jenny, you know where I live. You know I am not there to shove Jesus down your throat. I just want to help in any way I can." Seemingly it fell on deaf ears, until ten months later when she arrived on my doorstep late on a Sunday night. Greg had judged that she had not made enough money from prostitution that weekend so he threw her into the wall of their dingy apartment. I took her, broken and bleeding, to the A&E department at St. Vincent's Hospital, and who was there to receive us—Mary Maguire. Among other injuries, Greg had broken her arm, but that fracture led to the greatest break she could make. Jenny would not allow me to call the police, but she did let me call Vera and Jack. Hearing more bad news from me on the end of the phone, those wonderful parents jumped in their car at 10:00 p.m. and drove 536 miles (858 km) all night to Sydney.

The last time I saw Jenny was the next morning in the hospital car park as I helped her get into her parent's car for the ten-hour drive home. I stayed in touch with the three of them for a while until it was clear that I represented chapters in their family's life from which they wanted to move on.

In preparation for this chapter, I risked contacting them again for the first time since 1993. I did not want to write this story without their permission. On arrival at her parents' home, Jenny, then aged twenty-nine, had been appointed a thirty-two-year-old drug and alcohol counselor to assist her. Daryl helped her get clean and sober and in the process saw beyond her very rough and tough exterior. He fell in love with her. As professional boundaries demand, he took a transfer to another city and had nothing to do with her for eighteen months. On transferring back, he met his now former client and twelve months later married her. They now have two daughters and a son. The eldest is about to graduate from high school. Vera died four years ago and Jack, a doting grandfather, lives with his loving family. Jenny works at an assisted living facility. She has been clean and sober for over twenty-one years. Nineteen years ago, the police rang and told Jenny that Greg had died from a shotgun wound in the apartment they once shared. Her name was still on the lease. "I have to tell you, Father, I was relieved he was gone." While Jenny and I were delighted to connect again over the phone, and she gave me permission to use the story you have just read, she commented that "it moved me to tears, Father—to realize how far I've come from those very dark days. But keep praying for us. We need all the help we can get." It was clear at the end of that conversation, and rightly so, that any ongoing contact would unfairly complicate their lives. Sometimes the most amazing of graces is to know when to let go.

For Jenny, her personal trauma did not have the last word in her life. How did a God of faithful love break through into her world of utter and tragic powerlessness? It came through the saving love in human form in extraordinary parents who kept coming back for more, and who seized the opportunity when it presented itself to rescue their child. They drove all night. It came in the love of a man who saw beyond the tough exterior and very complex story of his client, a story that transformed both of them. It has come in the love of a mother for her four children, three of whom are still living. It came through the Jesuits and a charge nurse at a hospital who were in the right places at the right times, doing what we could. It came through Annie, who did not stand outside Jenny's grief, but knew it from the inside, and so could give another grieving mother the greatest gifts of solidarity and hope. No wonder that from that day on I wanted Annie and Johnny and their family to become my friends too. And it came in the ministry of an alcoholic and homeless man who at 3:30 one morning said, "I can't help you, but I can take you to people who can."

With the eyes of faith and a heart of love, the trauma of death and pain can give way to trusting that some good, any good, can emerge from evil, and that life will prevail where death had been before.

CONCLUSION

Faith is not certainty. Doubts and questions are essential elements of contemporary religious faith. We just need to be sure that we are sincerely looking for answers to our queries. In my reflections, I have argued that our dialogue with atheists can be clarifying, as long as any dialogue is conducted with mutual respect. In secular and pluralistic democracies, we are all free to accept and reject any religious belief, as long as it respects the rule of law and the rights of others. While religion should never have the only or final say in society, believers have every right to bring their religious faith to bear on debates and discussions in regard to laws and social policies. Where a particular religious faith is held by the vast majority, it is not surprising that a country's laws continue to enshrine the majority's values, while always protecting the minority's right to dissent, to further debate the issues, and to protect everyone's human rights and the freedom not to believe.

Though many of the current aggressive atheists often view all Christian believers as being the same, we are not. Just as there are many and various sorts of atheisms, there are many and various sorts of Christians too. Catholicism, the largest single Christian denomination, for example, does not take the Bible literally, and we no longer see science as the enemy of faith. We do not have to choose between the two. They are asking different questions. Science works to explain how we came to be here. Religious faith asks why we are here, what meaning there is to existence.

For believers, the argument that creation has occurred by random chance is not satisfying, for it is also a significant leap of faith, into randomness. For many of us, the sheer balance within creation and the minute structures of nature argue for a purposeful design and a meaning to existence. To hold that the world and our lives are, in fact, meaningless, and that we are destined for personal and cosmic extinction is, for believers, alienating. For people of faith, religious experience lies at the heart of their belief. While some of our detractors argue it is a form of mental illness, an encounter with one's faith in God is one of the most crosscultural and crossgenerational experiences attested to both in recorded history and today.

The appeal to religious experience raises the reality that there are different ways of knowing and different types of evidence. Just as in science there are different, contested ways to know scientific truths, so there is a variety of ways to know God, based on experience, mediated through a community of faith, and with the evidence of how people's lives change and are enriched as a result. Rational knowledge comes in different ways, and not only through the scientific method of questioning, hypothesizing, testing the hypothesis, analyzing results, drawing conclusions, and communicating the results. We know and trust many results in regard to other human experiences because we have encountered or experienced them: love, forgiveness, beauty, and conscience just to name a few. Similarly, just because religious experience is not processed the same way that scientific knowledge is, does not make it any less rational. Depending on people's religious experiences and intuitive knowledge of God, images of God and structures around a shared belief have developed. For all the great things religions have contributed to the human community, there is no escaping that some of the consequences of religious belief and doctrine have been, and are, criminal in what they have wreaked upon the created order and the human family. It is important to note that humanity has also suffered grievously under atheistic regimes. There is enough blame to go around for all ideologies.

While religion has played a disgraceful role in justifying war, no systematic analysis of the causes of war concludes that religion is the only and primary motivation for war. Ideology is born of greed for land or resources, and political power within cultures, tribes, and between nations. Even though some of our critics can quote texts from the Old and New Testaments, the Qur'an, and other sacred texts as positive proof that religion is inherently violent, it all depends on how one reads these texts, sees them in their historical context, and interprets them today. The vast majority of religious believers might hold to scriptures that, in part, speak of violence, but they live peacefully and agreeably with their neighbors. Terrorists use all sorts of ideologies to justify their criminal actions, religious or otherwise. Given that there are around 6.5 billion religious believers in the world, it is wrong to say that the evil behavior of a fraction of 1 percent of them represents all of us and what we believe.

By making a helpful distinction between truth and fact, Catholics, along with most other Christian churches, read the Bible as a library of books, with varying styles and importance that contain some facts, but are primarily about religious truths. Many mainstream Christians hold that these truths are tested and contested against the ongoing revelation and work of the Holy Spirit—promised to us in John 16:13—through history, science, theology, philosophy, biblical studies, politics, and social and religious experiences.

In this context, Christians affirm that Jesus did not simply and only come to die a grisly death to appease an angry God, but that he came to live, so that through his life, death, and resurrection, all of us might know of our dignity and redemption as individuals, and as a human family. For whatever else happened in and through the resurrection of Jesus, we know a timid group of ill-educated men and women from a poor outpost of the Roman Empire were emboldened to go out and change the world of their day, in many cases being prepared to die for Christ. Today, Christianity is at its best when it follows Jesus' own example of preferentially loving the world's poor through our actions in regard to advocating for their just needs, as well as providing for their education, healthcare, welfare, and pastoral care. We are at our worst through the despicable behavior of a very few church personnel who have criminally abused children given into our care, and in the leaders who thought that the protection of the Church was more important than the rights and needs of the victims and survivors.

WHAT DOES IT ALL MEAN?

Whenever Christianity strays from Jesus' law regarding the love of God, neighbor, and self, we end up in trouble. This law is the litmus test through which all things must be judged, including our own religious words and actions. It is the guiding principle of our moral code, including how we use our wealth and property to serve the human family. Not that the loving thing to do is not, sometimes, also the hardest and toughest decision; it is just that our morality is not about laws and rules and social control, it is about the ability to learn from two thousand years of experience in trying to live out Christ's love in the world, not repeating our many and heinous mistakes, naming the things that hold us back from realizing our own potential, and serving others so they might realize their own freedom as children of God.

Motivated, therefore, by the knowledge we have from religious experience, Christian prayer is about being utterly practical. It is not about heaven alone, it is about heaven on earth as well. It is not just about saving my soul, but being on mission to the world. And if we have stopped praying, then maybe it is time to start again, or go deeper still, so that we can be the most compassionate, hopeful, joyful, grateful, and forgiving person possible.

By living out this mission to pray, our lives that flow from it would change the world for the better. Furthermore, we would enable others not only to understand what faith and life mean to believers, for they would see it in our actions.

NOTES

PART I: THE CASE FOR FAITH

2. THE COMMON GROUND

1. Eugenio Scalfari and Pope Francis, "The Pope: How the Church Will Change," *La Repubblica*, October 1, 2013.

3. FREEDOM TO BELIEVE AND NOT BELIEVE

2. Pope Benedict XVI, *Meeting of the Holy Father Benedict XVI with the Clergy of the Dioceses of Belluno-Feltre and Treviso*, Tuesday, July 24, 2007.

3. See John C. Polkinghorne, *Science and Theology: An Introduction* (Minneapolis: Fortress Press, 1998), 75. Sam Harris, *The Moral Landscape: How Science Can Determine Human Values* (New York: Free Press, 2001), 161; "Obituaries: The Rev. Arthur Peacocke," *Telegraph*, October 25, 2006; and Sir Ernst Chain, in his public lecture "Social Responsibility and the Scientist in Modern Western Society," University of London, February, 1970.

4. Richard Dawkins, *River out of Eden: A Darwinian View of Life* (Grand Rapids: Zondervan, 1995), 131–32.

5. Colm Tóibín, interview with Geraldine Doogue, "Compass with Geraldine Doogue," Australian Broadcasting Commission, October 20, 2013.

6. Pope Benedict XVI, *Creation and Evolution: A Conference with Pope Benedict XVI in Castel Gandolfo* (San Francisco: Ignatius Press, 2008).

7. Interview with Simon Mayo, BBC Five, December 2, 2005.

8. Steven Katz, "Language, Epistemology and Mysticism," in *Mysticism and Philosophical Analysis*, ed. Steven Katz (New York: Oxford University Press, 1978). R. Woods, ed., *Understanding Mysticism* (Garden City, NY: Doubleday, 1980), 259.

9. William James, *The Varieties of Religious Experience* (Cambridge, MA: Harvard University Press, 1985).

10. Daniel Madigan, "When Experience Leads to Different Beliefs," *The Way Supplement* 92 (1998): 72–73.

11. Terence Kelly, *Reason and Religion in an Age of Science* (Adelaide: ATF Press, 2007), 162.

12. Father Placido Erzodain, *Archbishop Romero, Martyr of Salvador* (New York: Orbis Books, 1981).

13. The words are attributed to Monsignor Oscar Romero and often called the "Romero Prayer"; they were written by Bishop Ken Untener in honor of Romero in 1979.

PART II: CHALLENGES TO FAITH

4. RELIGION AND WAR

1. Meic Pearse, *The Gods of War: Is Religion the Primary Cause of Violent Conflict?* (Downers Grove, IL: InterVarsity Press, 2007).

2. Fareed Zakaria, "Let's Be Honest, Islam Has a Problem Right Now," *Washington Post* editorial, Oct. 9, 2014, http://www.washingtonpost.com/opinions/fareed-zakaria-islam-has-a-problem-right-now-but-heres-why-bill-maher-is-wrong/2014/10/09/b6302a14-4fe6-11e4-aa5e-7153e466a02d_story.html.

3. Sam Harris, "10 Myths—and 10 Truths—about Atheism," (blog), Dec. 24, 2006, https://www.samharris.org/blog/item/10-myths-and-10-truths-about-atheism.

4. Clifford Geertz, "Religion as a Cultural System," in *The Interpretation of Cultures: Selected Essays* (London: Fontana Press, 1993), 87–125.

5. FAITH, RELIGION, AND CHILD SEXUAL ABUSE

5. Pope Francis speaking to journalists on his plane following a high-profile visit to the Middle East in May, 2016. See Paul Sims, "Is Pope Francis Doing Enough to Address Clerical Child Abuse?" (blog) *New Humanist*, May 2, 2014, https://newhumanist .org.uk/articles/4666/is-pope-francis-doing-enough-to-address-clerical-child-abuse.

6. Homily of Pope Francis given at a Mass in the chapel of the Domus Sanctae Marthae with a group of clergy sex abuse victims: http://w2.vatican.va/content/francesco/en/cotidie/2014/documents/papa-francesco-cotidie_20140707_vittime-abusi.html.

6. IS THE BIBLE FACT OR FICTION?

7. Bernard Lonergan, *Method in Theology* (New York: Herder and Herder, 1972).

8. Richard Dawkins, *The God Delusion* (New York: Mariner Books, 2008), 51.

7. THE HISTORICAL JESUS

9. Epistles x. 96, cited in Frederick F. Bruce, *Jesus and Christian Origins Outside the New Testament* (Grand Rapids, MI: Eerdmans, 1974), 25; Gary R. Habermas, *The Historical Jesus: Ancient Evidence for the Life of Christ* (Joplin, MO: College Press, 1996), 198.

10. Lucian, *The Death of Peregrine*, in *The Works of Lucian of Samosata*, tran. H. W. Fowler and F. G. Fowler, 4 vols. (Oxford: Clarendon, 1949), 4:11–13, cited in Habermas, *The Historical Jesus*, 206.

10. WOMEN'S LEADERSHIP

11. Pope John Paul II, *Mulieris Dignitatem*, https://www.ewtn.com/library/PAPALDOC/JP2MULIE.HTM.

12. Pope Francis, Apostolic Exhortation *Evangelii Gaudium*, November 24, 2013, nos. 103–4.

13. Catholic New Service, "Italian Cardinal Willing to Re-examine Delicate Church Positions," *AmericanCatholic.org*, http://www.americancatholic.org/features/johnpaulii/transition/CardinalsMartini.asp.

14. Emil A. Wcela, "Why Not Women?" *America*, Oct. 1, 2012, http://americamagazine.org/issue/5152/article/why-not-women.

15. Joshua J. McElwee, "Vatican Spokesman: Female Cardinals 'Theoretically Possible,'" *National Catholic Reporter*, Nov. 4, 2013, http://ncronline.org/blogs/ncr-today/vatican-spokesperson-women-cardinals-theoretically-possible.

16. Letter of Father Joseph Tappiener, SJ, [South Australian Mission] to the Father General of the Jesuits, October 30, 1872 in *Letters and Documents in 19th Century Australian Catholic History*, ed. Brian Condon (Adelaide: College of Advanced Education Press, 1983).

11. THE CHALLENGE OF THE GOSPEL

17. Christopher Hitches, "Mommie Dearest: Pope Francis Will Make Mother Teresa—a Fanatic, a Fundamentalist, and a Fraud—a Saint," *Slate*, Dec. 18, 2015, http://www.slate.com/articles/news_and_politics/fighting_words/2003/10/mommie_dearest.html.

18. As quoted by Christopher Hitchens in *The Missionary Position: Mother Teresa in Theory and Practice* (Brooklyn: Verso, 1995), 11.

19. Mother Teresa, *Mother Teresa: Come Be My Light*, ed. Brian Kolodiejchuk (New York: Random House, 2006), 149, 192–93.

20. James Martin, "A Saint's Dark Night," *New York Times*, editorial, Aug. 29, 2007, http://www.nytimes.com/2007/08/29/opinion/29martin.html.

12. RELIGION, POLITICS, AND LAW

21. Richard Dawkins, "A Very Atheist Christmas," *Washington Post*, December 21, 2011.

22. See Michael Amalfitano, "Hollywood Ups and Downs," *LA Weekly*, December 18, 1998, 28.

23. Andrew Murray, "Battle of the Books," *New Statesman*, July 31, 2006.

24. Charles Taylor, "The Politics of Recognition," *Philosophical Arguments* (Cambridge, MA: Harvard University Press, 1995), 225–56.

25. See http://www.catholicpeacefellowship.org/wp/wordpress/resources/1974-cpf-statement-on-abortion/.

26. James Martin, SJ, "Dorothy Day and Abortion: A New Conversation Surfaces," *America*, July 1, 2011, http://americamagazine.org/content/all-things/dorothy-day-and-abortion-new-conversation-surfaces.

27. Robert Ellsberg, ed., *All the Way to Heaven: The Selected Letters of Dorothy Day* (Milwaukee: Marquette University Press, 2010).

28. Dorothy Day, "Beyond Politics," *The Catholic Worker*, November 1949, 1, 2, 4, http://www.catholicworker.org/dorothyday/articles/166.pdf.

PART III: THE GOD OF LOVE AND THE PROBLEM OF EVIL

13. BELIEF IN TIMES OF TRAGEDY

1. Tracey Leonard, *The Full Catastrophe* (Mahwah, NJ: HiddenSpring, 2010), 141ff.

17. ST. IGNATIUS LOYOLA (1491–1556)

2. Hugh Mackay, *The Good Life: What Makes a Life Worth Living?* (Sydney: Macmillan Australia, 2013), 12ff.

3. Ignatius of Loyola, "Prayer of Generosity," translated and adapted by Daniel Madigan, SJ.

19. WHAT OF MIRACLES?

4. Brian Doyle, *Leaping: Revelations and Epiphanies* (Chicago: Loyola Press, 2003), 25ff.

5. *Bruce Almighty*, screenplay by Steve Koren and Mark O'Keefe, rewrite by Steve Oedekerk. (Universal City, CA: Shady Acres Entertainment, 2002).

PART IV: LIFETIME LESSONS ON PRAYER

23. WHEN PRAYER IS PERSONAL

1. Ryan McKay, "Hallucinating God? The Cognitive Neuropsychiatry of Religious Belief and Experience," *Evolution and Cognition* 10, no. 1 (2004): 114–25.

2. "Names of God," http://www.smilegodlovesyou.org/names.html.

3. George Santayana, *The Life of Reason; or, the Phases of Human Progress: Introduction and Reason in Common Sense* (Ukraine: Leopold Classic Library, 2016).

INDEX